Preparing for Mediation

PREPARING

for

MEDIATION

A Practical Guide

Second Edition

GREG STONE

PINK UNICORN
PUBLISHING

Pink Unicorn Publishing
4607 Lakeview Canyon Road, #230
Westlake Village, CA 91361

© 2012, 2019 by Pink Unicorn Publishing

First Edition 2012
Second Edition 2019

Originally published by Pink Unicorn Publishing, 2012

ISBN (paperback): 978-0-9754397-5-3

Pink Unicorn Publishing thanks Tracy and Lindsay Stone for the cover and interior design.

Printed in the United States of America

To the peacemakers and mediators
who have helped develop
the alternative dispute resolution profession

Contents

ONE
Opening Remarks   1

TWO
Introduction to Conflict   3

THREE
Convening   9

FOUR
Mediator Selection   19

FIVE
Responses to Conflict   29

SIX
Your Story   35

SEVEN
Assessing Conflict   41

EIGHT
Faulty Perceptions   57

NINE
Communication   67

TEN
Discovery   75

ELEVEN
Managing Deception   81

TWELVE
The Hostile Party   89

THIRTEEN
Revenge   95

FOURTEEN
Stakeholders   105

FIFTEEN
Mining for Interests   107

SIXTEEN
Making Decisions   115

SEVENTEEN
Negotiation   131

EIGHTEEN
Managing Power   139

NINETEEN
Use of Power   157

TWENTY
Apology   169

TWENTY-ONE
Forgiveness   189

TWENTY-TWO
Impasse   201

TWENTY-THREE
Closing   213

TWENTY-FOUR
Closing Remarks   221

Notes   225

ONE

Opening Remarks

IF YOU ARE embroiled in a dispute that has escalated, there is a good chance you will be involved in litigation. Most likely, you are headed to trial. Yet there is a high probability that before you reach the courtroom you will negotiate a settlement agreement that resolves the conflict. A high percentage of disputes that give rise to lawsuits are resolved before trial; attorneys may negotiate on behalf of clients to resolve the lawsuit or the dispute may be resolved in *mediation*.

In order to maximize the satisfaction you will achieve in your negotiation, you will need to spend time preparing. Your results in negotiation, just like results in athletics, depend on preparation. All too often people spend considerable time and money preparing for trial but far too little time preparing for mediation. They put energy into the fight rather than the fix.

Paradoxically, mediation requires *more* extensive client preparation than litigation. As a mediator, I frequently encounter parties who arrive unprepared, lacking fundamental knowledge of the process. They arrive uncertain about their role. They are not sure how they will achieve the success they desire.

Preparing for Mediation was designed to solve this problem. The guide will help you and your attorney prepare for successful mediation. Even if your dispute has not yet escalated into a lawsuit, you will find that this book provides valuable assistance for resolving conflicts.

Mediation addresses the full range of human challenges. This makes simplifying the process a challenge. If we abbreviate the description of the process too much, vital information is omitted. On the other hand, parties in a dispute find that time is at a premium: if preparation takes too long, they abandon the preliminary work. For this reason, *Preparing for Mediation* offers a comprehensive yet streamlined approach that can be completed in a reasonable amount of time.

Different preparation strategies exist. Your attorney may guide you through the process, directing your attention to selected prompts. Or you may read the entire text, respond to all prompts, and then meet with your attorney to discuss your responses.

At the outset, you will want to discuss two legal concepts with your counsel: *attorney-client privilege* and *mediation confidentiality*. These concepts concern your right to maintain confidentiality with regard to your preparation work. Most discussions with your attorney are privileged communications. This allows you to engage in frank exchanges while preparing for trial or mediation. In addition, most jurisdictions have statutes that regulate mediation confidentiality; these statutes protect verbal communications and written materials prepared specifically for mediation.

Confidentiality is vital for mediation success; legislators and courts recognize its importance. As statutes vary from venue to venue, however, it is important to discuss privilege and confidentiality with your attorney, thereby insuring that your notes and responses to the prompts in this guide remain protected.[1]

Welcome to mediation preparation. I encourage you to put forth your best effort, as your preparation will be well rewarded in the satisfaction you derive from a negotiated outcome.

⤝⤞

Discuss attorney-client privilege with your attorney.

Discuss mediation confidentiality with your attorney.

Discuss, with your attorney, how you will best use this guide in resolving your particular dispute.

TWO

Introduction to Conflict

LET'S GET STARTED. In each chapter, key mediation concepts will be introduced, followed by prompts for you to consider. Document your responses in a personal journal, labeling and identifying the material as "work product prepared exclusively for mediation."

We start with an introduction to the basics: *What is conflict? What is mediation? What are my options?*

CONFLICT

Conflict can play a negative role in our lives: it can ruin our health, happiness, and prosperity. But conflict can also result in growth that renders us wiser, happier, stronger, and more committed in our relationships. Typically, our experience with conflict depends on how skilled we are in managing and resolving disputes.

In addition, our views affect the consequences we experience: if we view conflict as an opportunity to increase understanding and collaboration, the process may be therapeutic and uplifting. If we are confident in our conflict resolution skills, we experience more positive outcomes. Therefore, it makes sense to assess your conflict resolution skills and your attitude toward conflict.

❦

Do you feel you can make a difference in the outcome of this dispute? Why or why not?

Do you possess skills needed to engage in mediation?

What new skills will you need to acquire?

What vital skills will others provide on your behalf?

Are you prepared to take advantage of opportunities to resolve conflict?

If you are invited to mediate, will you accept the invitation? Why or why not?

CONFLICT RESOLUTION OPTIONS

In order to better understand the advantages mediation offers, you will want to understand the range of dispute resolution options available. Mediation is not the only approach to resolving disputes. Figure One illustrates major conflict resolution approaches.

On the left side of the chart, we find less formal approaches; on the right, more formal approaches. Options on the left honor party self-determinism, while options on the right call on a third party—a judge, jury or elder—to render a decision or verdict. Mediation, located near the center of the continuum, blends informal and formal techniques in a facilitated negotiation that seeks a resolution the parties agree upon.

Someone may arrive at mediation having failed to achieve resolution using a less formal process. They may have tried to "talk it out" and failed. Or they may arrive at mediation after employing a more formal process. For example, they may have filed a lawsuit but now wish to attempt mediation before trial commences.

⟡

Have you attempted to resolve this dispute using other processes?

What did you try? What happened?

Are you still involved in another process?

CONFLICT RESOLUTION APPROACHES

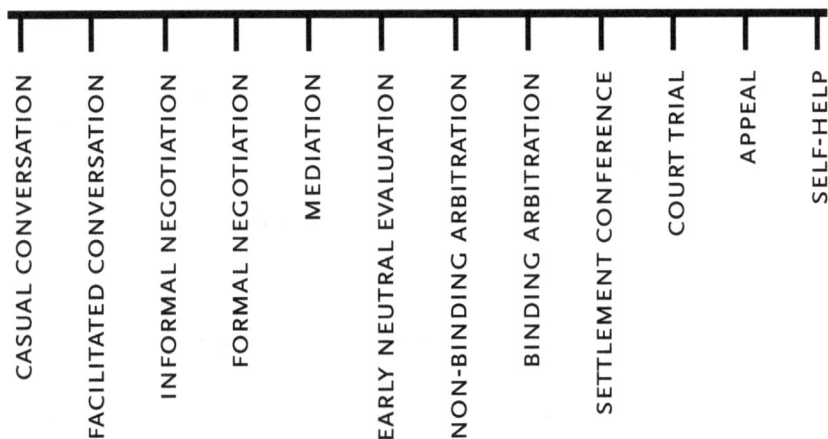

Fig. 1 Conflict Resolution Approaches

MEDIATION & THE CAUSES OF CONFLICT

Mediation seeks to handle the underlying causes of conflict. It is a flexible and creative process that addresses the psychological and emotional aspects of relationship—as well as legal concerns such as contracts, rights, liability and damages. A court trial rarely explores interpersonal issues simmering beneath the surface, whereas mediation excels in addressing substance *and* relationship. Mediation flexibility increases the opportunity for reconciliation.

Typically, your lawyer will accompany you through the process. She often introduces the dispute on your behalf in a mediation brief and/or in an oral presentation. As the process advances, you are encouraged to take an increasingly active role.

While negotiation regarding substantive issues (deal points) plays a central role in mediation, re-negotiating the relationship is often just as important. The manner in which parties have treated one another is frequently an issue that needs to be resolved.

In this dispute, must interpersonal relationship issues be resolved before you resolve issues regarding substance?

What interpersonal issues will need to be addressed?

NO PENALTY, NO DOWNSIDE

If mediation reaches an impasse and you are unable to achieve a collaborative agreement, you are free to end the process without penalty. You may return to litigation to seek a verdict. Thus, a decision to mediate typically has little or no downside.

Do you consider you will be taking a risk if you decide to mediate?

Describe the risk, if any.

THE TRIAL EXPERIENCE

A *court trial* is a formal process with extensive procedural rules. A judge or a jury determines the outcome — the verdict. There are times when we value a third-party decision. For example, we may want to distance ourselves from the outcome, particularly when it appears our adversary will be unable to let go and end the conflict. In such situations, a party may value a verdict over which they have little or no control. They may hope the other party will redirect their hostility and blame toward the court.

$$\backsim$$

In this dispute, is it vital that the other party redirect blame and hostility toward a third-party decision maker, such as the court? Describe the circumstances.

LITIGATION EXPECTATIONS

Trials rarely provide a high level of satisfaction. The trial-based narrative usually does not match the party's version of what happened. In the courtroom, the jury hears a narrative account constrained by legal procedures. As a result, parties often feel unable to make their concerns fully known. The idea of *having your day in court to tell your story* very often becomes an unrealized dream.

For this reason, litigation outcomes rarely satisfy party expectations, even for those who win. Party satisfaction may also be diminished by time lost and money spent. Stress and worry exact an emotional toll. Victory may be rendered bittersweet by embarrassing public exposure of private matters.

In contrast, during mediation, parties are encouraged to speak in depth, candidly, knowing there is a degree of confidentiality. They are encouraged to speak not only about the facts of the case, but also about feelings, motives, concerns, and interests. A subtle shift from attorney presentation to client participation takes place.

Mediation fosters party involvement and collaboration, whereas in a trial parties have little or no direct interaction. In mediation, parties help determine the outcome, which contributes to their satisfaction.

In addition, mediators have found success more likely when parties are encouraged to address their relationship in a flexible process. Once relationship challenges are overcome, they are better prepared to engage in collaborative problem solving. The resulting collaborative outcomes that honor party self-determinism prove to be more durable. Parties are more likely to comply with the terms of a settlement they helped negotiate than with a trial verdict.

❧

Would you like an opportunity to tell your story?

Do you look forward to explaining what happened?

If you are prevented from telling your story of what happened in your own words, will you be upset?

Do you want to hear the other party's story?

Do you need to hear the other party's story?

Does the public exposure you will receive during a trial concern you?

Are you prepared for the mental and emotional stress of a trial?

How important is the opportunity to play a role in determining the outcome?

How comfortable are you with letting someone else (a judge or a jury) decide your future?

THREE

Convening

CONVENING ENCOMPASSES STEPS that mediators take to "get to the table" where parties can collaborate on finding a creative solution to a dispute. Typically, during a conflict, each party avoids working with the other party. In the convening stage, mediators seek to overcome barriers that prevent parties from coming together with their hearts and minds engaged in a search for solutions. At this stage, mediators seek to generate hope and inspire the feuding parties to mediate.

CONVENING CHALLENGES

Though a trial judge may recommend mediation, and though you may agree to attend, you may not be committed to active participation. Hope is often lacking. Parties arrive with a wait-and-see attitude, without a personal understanding of *why* they should mediate. They harbor an unstated question: "What's in it for me?"

Previously, you may have vowed never to work with that other party; strong motivation is needed to overcome this prior decision. In some instances, the cost of litigation alone may motivate you to abandon your previous vow. Or you may anticipate a jury will have little sympathy for your cause: you sense you will be better off negotiating in spite of previous vows not to do so. This means you may arrive at mediation upset with the idea that you must now work with your nemesis. Your heart is not fully invested in the process. You may even hesitate to go forward.

In this situation, a mediator can help you evaluate the negative consequences of refusing to mediate. In many cases, a mediator presents practical reasons to mediate, yet fails to generate hope. Instead, convening often begins with the recognition that the alternatives are unattractive.

CONSEQUENCES

Unresolved conflict can be extremely destructive, exacting a tremendous financial, physical, emotional, psychological, and spiritual toll. Left unresolved, conflict can render us ill with its steady drumbeat of stress and uncertainty. We may experience sleepless nights, loss of appetite (or compulsive eating), and obsessive worry. Our troubled mind may drift from important tasks to fantasies of making our nemesis suffer the pain we feel. Bad humor may cloud our mood, leading to upsets with those with whom we have no quarrel. Relationships may suffer. We may sink into depression, fearing our future will be compromised by the adverse consequences of our conflict.

As our focus narrows to the fight before us, we miss opportunities. We lose faith in our fellow man. As a result, we fail to notice uplifting expressions of kindness aimed in our direction. Animosity turns inward: we suffer guilt and wonder if our flaws are the cause of our troubles. We consider an apology, but our stomach churns at the thought of humbling ourselves, so we shore up our defenses and vow to fight to the end. We daydream of the painful revenge we hope to exact.

Careers may be damaged; families may suffer harm. Domestic tranquility may become compromised when we vent conflict-driven frustration. Consumed with the struggle, we may suffer nightmares in which our adversary launches violent attacks against us.

Thus, we must carefully consider our current path and the consequences that will accrue. We must assess the pros and cons of continuing the fight and assess the costs of continued conflict. How do these costs compare to mediation? Unless we truly understand the stakes, we will fail to properly value the hard work needed to resolve the conflict.

&

List pros and cons of allowing the conflict to escalate.

What is likely to happen if the conflict is not resolved?

List pros and cons of mediation.

What consequences might prevent you from mediating?

Do you imagine the other party will agree to mediate?

Why might they try mediation?

Why might they refuse mediation?

RISK REWARD ANALYSIS

A risk-reward picture takes shape. If you have more to lose than to gain, you will be unlikely to convene mediation. Most parties, however, see considerable potential gain with little risk. The downside is minimal: if the conciliatory process fails, you resume the fight. Agreeing to mediate is not an irrevocable commitment to a resolution; rather, it is a commitment to *work on* crafting an amicable resolution.

Too often parties refuse to mediate without adequately evaluating pros and cons. Too often this is a response to unsettled emotions or a desire to avoid confrontation. The longer a conflict persists, however, the greater the risk: relationships suffer; costs skyrocket; the conflict comes to define the party; hearts harden; accumulated hurts fester; desire for revenge festers; hope gives way to despair.

The earlier you convene, the better. But what if you are not yet emotionally prepared to convene? A realistic appraisal of adverse consequences may motivate you to come to the table. During the early stages of escalation, consequences may not yet be sufficiently clear to motivate action. In this situation, a mediator helps you evaluate the value of convening and helps you better understand the cost of delay.

$\approx$

Analyze the pros and cons of mediation in greater detail.

What might be the consequences of a delay?

How might you prepare yourself emotionally?

What might motivate the other party to mediate?

What insights might you want to share with the mediator in order to facilitate convening?

ACCEPTING HELP

It can be difficult to accept outside assistance; our culture prizes self-reliance. The nature of conflict, however, often dictates that we call on a third-party mediator. This is not due to a failure of individual enterprise, integrity, or skill, but rather reflects the unique interpersonal dynamics of conflict.

It can be nearly impossible for individuals locked in opposition to disengage on their own. You may find it difficult to reach out to your adversary: convening seems futile. You worry that any willingness to mediate will be mistaken for weakness. Fear that you will be perceived as weak prevents you from participating in mediation. Besides, you muse, if conflict escalates, perhaps you can defeat the other party.

Nonetheless, in spite of your reticence, a judge may recommend you make a good-faith attempt to settle the dispute. Your lawyer may also recommend mediation, or an influential elder or authority figure in your family or community may suggest you seek harmony. At this point, you usually need the help of a mediator to work through the challenging stage of convening.

Will a mediator be needed to oversee and facilitate convening?

What will you need to do to "get to the table"?

Are you concerned you will appear weak? Why?

Has someone with authority recommended that you mediate?

What considerations or fears might inhibit your full commitment to participate in mediation?

POWER IMBALANCE

An inaccurate perception of power may delay convening mediation. A party with an inflated sense of power may believe they have no need to convene; they may assume there is no downside to their refusal. However, wielding power unwisely or arrogantly often surfaces unintended adverse consequences. The misuse of power damages relationships. A party can avoid this potential error by engaging in an accurate assessment of the conflict.

This power dynamic may play out in other ways. For example, one party may attempt to bring the other party to the table by raising a hypothetical adverse consequence that the reticent party might suffer. He promotes collaboration by painting a dark picture of the downside of continued conflict. The reticent party, however, usually sees the hypothetical downside as a veiled threat. The attempt to explain possible benefits by raising potential adverse consequences often backfires.

A mediator, however, may raise potential adverse consequences without being seen as threatening. He or she may ask, "What consequences might result from *your* actions? If you use power in this manner, are you certain there will be no unforeseen adverse consequences?" The mediator floats hypothetical scenarios, framing potential events in a way that avoids the perception of veiled threats.

❧

Do you anticipate that a power imbalance will delay convening?

What might convince the other party to temporarily set aside coercive power?

Have you overlooked your power to influence decisions?

Must you suspend your use of coercive power in order to collaborate?

MEDIATOR ASSISTANCE WITH CONVENING

You may find it difficult to imagine that a mediator will enjoy success when you have failed in your attempts to engage the opposing party in mediation. You might overlook just how difficult it is to sell an opponent on the benefits of mediation. Your pitch will be seen as self-serving, whereas a mediator, who has nothing to gain, can make an identical suggestion and find a receptive audience. The mediator is not hampered by a conflict of interest.

A mediator acknowledges that both you and your opponent want to know, "What's in this for me?" He helps parties recognize advantages and benefits in a matter-of-fact manner. If you balk, the mediator seeks to discover the source of your hesitation—without dismissing your interests. He helps you explore various scenarios and helps you move past barriers to convening. The mediator speaks with each party individually, encouraging them to participate. She may suggest that an opponent will agree to participate—*if the decision is mutual.* She floats the idea of reciprocal interest: "If I can generate interest on the part of the other party, will you consider taking part?" This approach overcomes the fear that a party will be seen as weak if they are the first to agree to convene. In this approach the mediator brings about a simultaneous and mutual decision to mediate.

Another fear may arise during convening. You may fear an agreement to convene is an unstated commitment to settle on terms you do not fully accept. The mediator allays this fear by stressing the voluntary nature of the process; he assures you he does not intend to force or coerce a settlement. You are allowed to accept or reject any settlement. You may walk away from the table. Mediation is voluntary and the risks are minimal.

This convening stage should not be skipped over lightly. Parties must be emotionally and mentally prepared to participate, or forward progress will be fleeting.

❧

Will you need a mediator's help to bring the other party to the table?

How might you help the mediator convince the other party to convene?

Will you need the mediator to help you understand the process and the possibilities?

What questions do you have regarding mediation?

SAVING FACE

"Face" is the need to be perceived in a positive manner. It is the need to be respected. When we honor Face, we recognize another's need to be admired, appreciated, and valued. When we tend to their esteem, we tend to their Face. Mediators help parties Save Face, Restore Face, and Protect Face.

When we suffer Face Loss, we experience confusion, embarrassment, and a sense of inferiority; our self-image is damaged. Face Loss results from put-downs, sarcasm, snide remarks, or actions that diminish our self-worth. When we are harmed or overpowered, we experience Face Loss.

People have a strong need to maintain a favorable self-image. They need the inner contentment that supplies the exterior confidence required to sustain quality relationships. When they suffer Face Loss, they shut down their interactions, which further exacerbates conflict. In their effort to Save Face, they may not even admit that conflict exists.

The need to Save Face is a common barrier to convening. If you must admit you have been unable to handle conflict, you may experience Face Loss. In your mind, only ineffective, incompetent, or weak people fail to resolve conflict. Or you may consider that you must always be loving and caring—thus, the presence of conflict signals that you are flawed, which creates Face Loss. Thus, the need to Save Face may not allow you to admit that a conflict must be addressed. This may be true for the other party as well.

For this reason, resistance to mediation often signals a need to Save Face. In response, a mediator proposes guidelines that Protect Face while framing conflict as normal. He explains that conflict resolution is not a remedy for our flaws but is rather a way that people equipped with advanced social skills work together. He tells the parties that in mediation we do not seek to repair shortcomings; rather, we seek to use our skills to reestablish harmony.

PREVIOUS FACE LOSS

In most conflicts, Face Loss looms large. Parties are certain previous disrespect cannot be forgiven. While issues regarding "the deal" might be amenable to resolution, Face Loss seems beyond remedy. Parties may be able to work around a contract breach, a failure to pay, a disputed boundary, a broken treaty, a salary dispute, or a barking dog—but insults and disrespect make mediation impossible. They protest, "There is no way I will sit down with *that* kind of person."

A Face Threat ends the convening conversation, especially if previous insults are glibly excused with the platitude: "We all say nasty things when we are upset." Instead, a mediator works to Restore Face. He may need to choreograph tentative apologies or mild expressions of regret. While such conciliatory moves are often needed, they should not place an emphasis on previous Face Loss. Instead, they should provide hope for future respect.

We might assume that a previous grave insult requires an equally weighty apology to jumpstart the dispute resolution process; instead, we discover the change in direction—from Face Threat to Face Saving—is what matters. An overly profuse apology at this stage appears unrealistic: it is not credible. The offended party can accept only a modicum of remorse as realistic. An overly grand gesture arouses suspicion.

Mediators face a challenge: how do they Restore Face and yet avoid additional Face Loss, which may occur if they point out previous Face Loss. They must avoid implying that a party was weak and vulnerable. For example, a preliminary apology may elicit a party's denial: "You embarrassed me? No way. I didn't even notice what you said. Forget about it. It's fine." The inner dialogue, however, mixes unexpressed resentment (over the past) with unexpressed gratitude (for the apology). Ironically, the offended party's desire to make their adversary grovel is offset by their need to deny they were vulnerable in the first place!

UNRECOGNIZED THREATS TO FACE

A party may express emotional defensiveness out of proportion to the substance of the conflict. In such cases, undetected Face Loss drives Face Saving behavior. The party hides their hurt and Protects Face with hostile stances. If a mediator is not careful, Face Loss will remain unrecognized and unacknowledged and will impede convening.

If this seems to be an overly fine-grained analysis, I assure you it is not. When it comes to Face, a mediator must perform as if he were an explosives expert disarming a bomb — it *does* matter which wire he disconnects.

☙

Will the need to Save Face inhibit efforts to convene?

Has Face Loss occurred?

What will you need to do to Restore Face so mediation can take place?

Will you need to discuss Saving Face with the mediator?

Will there be a need for a preliminary apology?

How will prior insults or disrespect be addressed?

THE MEDIATOR & FACE NEEDS

When one party represents a Face Threat to another, there is little chance of convening. In contrast, when a mediator honors Face, it prompts inner dialogue: "You [the other party] may not respect me, but the mediator does. So you [the other party] are wrong, I *do* have worth." Where previously there was only impasse, hope surfaces.

During the convening stage, the mediator may ask you to express your concerns regarding procedure. She may ask you to help design guidelines that promote safety and assuage fears. You may insist the other party stop calling you insulting names or yelling at you. You might express your initial fear of meeting jointly and request separate sessions — a form of shuttle diplomacy. The mediator will design a process that provides hope and safety.

⸙

What concerns might prevent the other party from coming to the table?

How might the mediator help the other party overcome those barriers?

What process guidelines are needed?

Do safety issues exist that should be brought to the mediator's attention?

Have you discussed guidelines and safety with your attorney?

Will it be necessary to avoid joint sessions at the beginning?

FOUR

Mediator Selection

IN MOST CASES, your attorney will select a mediator on your behalf. However, you will want to consult with your attorney and offer your thoughts on the type of mediator that best meets your needs.

MEDIATOR CHARACTER & STYLE

What characteristics will you value in a mediator? Preferences differ. In some cultures, a disinterested, neutral third party is preferred; in other cultures, a village elder or religious leader is chosen. In a business dispute, a distinguished late career professional may be the best choice. Young people may find a peer mediator best suited to the task. In other cases, parties choose the "expert from afar," the empathetic pastoral counselor or the seasoned diplomat.

Mediator styles vary. Retired judges may be evaluative; they may focus on "getting the deal done," offering opinions on settlement parameters. Other mediators may adopt a more facilitative style, guiding the process while leaving the settlement parameters to the parties. Transformative mediators nurture changes that heal relationships; they focus on personal growth, viewing settlement as a by-product of inner changes. Skilled mediators use all these styles, tailoring their approach to the specific dispute and its unique party needs.

A mediator may direct the process with a strong hand or allow parties to find their own way through trial and error. Some parties want an outcome that allows them to move on with their lives. Others prefer a less direct approach that fosters inner transformation and gradually overcomes barriers. A pragmatic party may seek immediate relief and a return to business-as-usual; others may seek more enduring outcomes based on transformation of long-term relationships.

✑

Describe the mediator characteristics you feel will best meet your needs.

Will an evaluative, facilitative, or transformative approach be best for this dispute? Do you need a mediator who exerts strong control or someone who is less directive? Why? Share your thoughts with your attorney.

What concerns do you anticipate the other party has regarding mediator selection?

MEDIATOR SUBJECT MATTER EXPERTISE

On occasion, a mediator will be chosen for her knowledge of a specific profession or industry. Industry-specific knowledge allows a mediator to quickly understand pertinent issues; familiarity with nomenclature, customs, and protocols may prove helpful. In your case, will the mediator need experience with a specific industry?

A word of caution: it would be an error to select a mediator with industry-specific knowledge in the hope she will render a verdict based on technical facts. Mediators do not deliver verdicts. If you desire a quasi-judicial ruling on the merit of technical facts, you may wish to seek an *early neutral evaluation* provided by a legal expert in your field.[1]

Typically, it makes more sense to assign greater weight to the mediator's ability to touch and transform hearts. In most instances, a technical question is not central to the conflict; rather, key questions regard relationship, ethics, and communication. Parties typically bring technical expertise to the table: they know their business. If a dispute truly pivots on technical issues, the parties would have jointly consulted an expert — *if* relationship problems had not prevented such collaboration. The barrier to reconciliation usually has to do with the relationship, not technical facts.

Technical issues may serve as smokescreens that hide personal issues. I have listened for hours as parties have debated proper industry protocol and their rights under the law — only to finally achieve a breakthrough when they revealed the *real* issue had to do with insult, face loss, and jealousy.

If one selects a mediator for technical or legal expertise and that expertise fails to satisfy both parties, the process hits an impasse. In contrast, when a mediator guides parties through difficult emotional, psychological, and spiritual terrain, the threat of impasse is lessened.

A mediator who is also a lawyer must avoid a predisposition to focus on legal issues when legal issues do not fully capture the conflict. What began as a relationship problem may have turned into a legal problem as a result of escalation; legal solutions may only postpone the day when the real causes of conflict surface.

At times a legal decision may be all you desire, but at other times your needs may differ. Share your concerns with your attorney. You may recognize that factors driving the conflict are not what they appear to be; you may suspect that an outcome based solely on legal issues will not endure; you may anticipate the conflict will resurface if relationship issues are not addressed. Keep your lawyer informed so the right mediator can be selected.

Will technical issues require specific expertise?

What qualities, skills, or experience will you emphasize in mediator selection?

Will a technical issue require the testimony of an expert?

Have technical issues masked underlying relationship problems?

Are you concerned that mediation will not focus on relationship?

MEDIATOR ASSISTANCE

Your legal rights may be central to your dispute; your lawyer may have researched issues and interpreted applicable law on your behalf. Opposing attorneys, however, may disagree with the analysis. As a result, a judge may be called upon to render a decision on the law. However, mediators do *not* function as judges and do *not* render legal decisions.

If you want to evaluate the strength of your case, you might have the mediator assume the role of a potential juror. He can pose hypothetical questions jurors might ask. Such clarifying questions provide valuable insights into how your story communicates. Previously, you might have imagined that your arguments were clear and indisputable; now you become aware of ambiguity. You may discover that, had you gone to trial, jurors might have responded in unanticipated ways. This may motivate you to participate fully in mediation.

In any event, mediation should not stall as a result of speculation as to how the law will be interpreted. If the process hangs up on opposing legal views, a *litigation risk analysis* might identify strengths and weaknesses.[2] Risk analysis assigns a probability of success at each branch on a litigation decision tree, then sums up the overall probability of trial success.

Few litigants actually complete a detailed analysis. Fortunately, completion is not always critical; the important lesson is that a trial involves risk. The unwarranted but common certainty of victory fades when probabilities are assigned. Perhaps for the first time, a party considers the consequences of an adverse outcome. They realize juries can be unpredictable: results are not always just or rational. Risk analysis focuses a party's attention on solving problems and repairing relationships rather than on defending legal theory.

Might litigation risk analysis help you better understand your alternatives to mediation?

Discuss with your attorney how you might move beyond an impasse created by differing views of the law.

What questions might you pose to a potential juror to see if he or she understands your claim?

What would you like to learn from a potential juror?

Will aspects of your case be difficult to convey clearly?

AGREEING ON MEDIATOR SELECTION

Your choice of a mediator does not end the selection process, as both parties must agree. Often, the other party rejects a mediator simply because *you* select her. It may be necessary to engage in a back-and-forth negotiation. It helps to know *why* you want a particular mediator so you can explain your decision to the other side.

In addition, mediators must disclose all possible conflicts of interest. Any relationship that raises doubt regarding impartiality must be disclosed. Even the *appearance* of a conflict of interest may raise doubts, forcing a mediator to step aside. If a conflict of interest later emerges, the mediator should offer to decline the assignment. Parties must decide if a change is warranted.

In rare circumstances, however, you may consider that a prior relationship between the mediator and the opposing party offers an advantage. The prior relationship may allow the mediator to convey bad news or difficult information to your opponent that would not be accepted if the news were delivered by an adversary or by a neutral person they did not know.

Consult with your attorney regarding how you will address mediator conflicts of interest.

Are there any current conflicts of interest that should be made known?

Do you anticipate a need for a pre-convening conference with the mediator?

Will you need to impart information to the mediator to help her design the process?

Why might the other party reject your choice of a mediator?

MEDIATION MINDSET

An inherent tension exists between litigation and mediation. In litigation, we seek to destroy our opponent's credibility and maximize the verdict in our favor. In mediation, we seek to establish trust so we can collaborate and pursue a mutually satisfactory outcome. A dramatic shift in mindset and skills must take place as we change the process.

A dispute played out in court typically starts with a lawsuit (complaint) that alleges bad behavior by another party. It usually includes a claim for compensation to be paid to the harmed party. This is followed by a response from the accused party challenging the credibility of the party who filed the original complaint and disputing the validity of their claim.

Then, during the discovery phase (see Chapter 10), lawyers attempt to unearth evidence that will impeach the opponent.[3] They employ depositions and interrogatories in the search for evidence. In pre-trial motions parties request rulings that limit evidence their adversary can present. As the financial and emotional investment increases, parties may become increasingly fixated on defeating one another. Hostility escalates. Collaboration seems less and less likely—yet collaboration is the approach called for in mediation. Thus, the litigation process moves parties away from a mediation mindset.

The transition from litigation to mediation is analogous to driving a hundred-miles-per hour on an icy road and slamming on the brakes. One may feel a dramatic loss of control. For this reason, the mediator proceeds slowly, and guides parties as they shift gears to facilitated negotiation.

The shift may also be difficult for attorneys. In litigation, they have a duty to provide zealous advocacy, and clients usually desire such unwavering support. Zealous advocacy, however, does not mean unfettered legal warfare; the best advocacy often results in a settlement achieved through persuasion rather than intimidation. While a party may have retained an attorney for his aggressive demeanor, in mediation the attorney must generate trust. As an aggressive demeanor can inhibit trust-building, the attorney must make a major adjustment.

In litigation, the opponent's concerns may be ignored or actively opposed, but in mediation, a party must give his opponent's concerns serious consideration. If a party demonstrates, even unintentionally, that they are dismissive of their opponent's concerns, the process shuts down.

Another possible dynamic warrants consideration. Parties may be motivated to extend an olive branch simply to avoid the adversarial demeanor of opposing counsel. In this situation, the adversarial demeanor *promotes* dialogue. It is uncommon, however, for aggression to bring about conciliation; an aggressive demeanor usually motivates the opposing party to fight to the bitter end.

Research verifies that litigating most often results in less favorable outcomes for the client.[4] The plaintiff who wins typically receives less than was previously offered in settlement talks; the defendant who loses pays more than he would have paid in settlement. Thus, you are more likely to satisfy your interests through collaboration than through a verdict. This makes the challenging shift from litigation to mediation worthwhile.

❦

What difficulty, if any, do you anticipate if you were to shift from litigation to mediation?

What do you expect will be the greatest challenge?

Discuss the shift with your attorney.

Do you agree with your attorney on strategy?

How will you handle disagreements should they surface?

Do you anticipate that the other party will shift to mediation?

ATTORNEY STYLE

Attorney styles vary: some exert strong control and direct the process; some are client-centered, following the client's direction; others are collaborative.[5] Prior to mediation, discuss with your lawyer how you plan to work together.

❦

How would you characterize your working relationship with your attorney?

Will you need to discuss concerns regarding mediation in more depth?

BRIEFING THE MEDIATOR

Attorneys often submit mediation briefs that describe the conflict. They work with the mediator to schedule and plan the process.[6] At this convening stage, you will be encouraged to disclose past violence, threats exchanged, or other risk factors that may warrant convening in separate sessions and which allow you to remain at a safe distance. Mediation is not a rote process; every conflict presents unique demands, so be sure to share your concerns.

Will your attorney submit a mediation brief?

Is safety a concern?

How will you brief the mediator regarding your procedural concerns?

Will mediation need to take place with the parties in separate rooms? Why?

FIVE

Responses to Conflict

IN MANY INSTANCES, the manner in which we respond to conflict is unique to the situation; our response is appropriate to the circumstances. However, at times, we respond without much thought or reason. We greet conflict in a habitual manner—even though in the past our habits have resulted in failures.

Conflict triggers emotions that blur reason, resulting in patterned responses. After we react out of habit, we often fail to recognize how our patterned response contributed to subsequent adverse events. We consider the poor outcome to be the inevitable consequence of conflict. Thus, we need to become aware of our habitual responses. Success in conflict resolution requires an ability to respond to the unique aspects of a situation. As much as possible, we must act in the present.

✧

When confronted with opposition and conflict, what is your typical response?

Do you feel you are in control when you are involved in a conflict?

YOUR PERSONAL APPROACH TO CONFLICT

Assess the ways you habitually cede conscious control to patterned, pre-programmed responses. Do you seek to control, dominate, coerce, or manipulate others? Do you experience an urge to defeat and crush the other party, literally or metaphorically? Do you marshal your power in order to compete? Or do you strive to restore harmony at any cost, becoming subservient and deferential, banishing all signs of opposition? Do you appease or accommodate and sacrifice personal needs? Do you easily abandon your point of view? Do you seek to compromise and "divide the pie"? Or do you seek to escape from the situation and avoid conflict?

When it comes to responses to conflict, the two primary opposing focuses are *concern for self-interest* and *concern for others' interests*. If we are primarily concerned with satisfying our own needs, we tend to compete, perhaps in a dominating, coercive, or manipulative manner. On the other hand, if we are willing to sacrifice or defer our interests, we tend to accommodate the needs of the other party.[1]

Let's look at the diagram of habitual responses. If a party focuses on satisfying their interests and competing, they fall on the top left of the scale. If their focus is on satisfying the interests of others, they seek to accommodate. This position is found on the bottom right. When a party seeks to compromise, they balance their needs against the needs of the other party. Those who desire to maximize the satisfaction of both their needs *and* the needs of the other party seek to collaborate.

We may "dance" with someone whose habitual response to conflict compliments our own response. For example, a competitive person might form a relationship with an accommodating person. Habit often fosters such non-optimum symbiotic relationships.

Perhaps the most common response is *avoidance*. We abandon our needs *and* the needs of the other in an effort to circumvent a collision of interests. We decide it just isn't worth the fight. At times this response is valid: the cost of conflict may be so extreme the best solution is avoiding a clash and foregoing satisfaction. Neither party satisfies their interests, and neither suffers great harm. While at times avoidance makes sense, it is not optimum.

Compromise is a middle path chosen when we are not prepared to abandon our interests *and* we are not prepared to force the other party to abandon their interests. Each party foregoes a portion of their interests while satisfying a portion; each suffers limited defeat and enjoys limited victory. Though we might consider compromise a partial win, it also represents partial loss. Compromise thus retains a slight feel of avoidance.

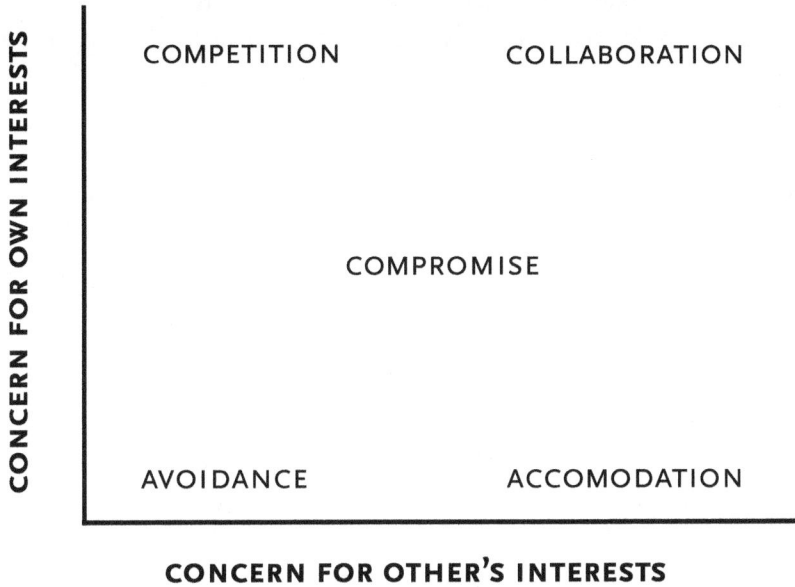

COMPETITION   COLLABORATION

CONCERN FOR OWN INTERESTS

COMPROMISE

AVOIDANCE   ACCOMODATION

CONCERN FOR OTHER'S INTERESTS

Figure 2. Responses to Conflict

Mediators strive to bring about *collaboration* in which the interests of both parties are satisfied with creative solutions. Collaboration is not based on "dividing the pie" but rather on "expanding the pie" through exploration of interests. Parties who collaborate move to "the same side of the table" in problem-solving mode.

While collaboration provides the greatest satisfaction in most cases, each approach (avoidance, competition, accommodation, compromise, collaboration) is valid in specific situations. Ideally, we want to master the skill of employing a wide range of responses, as adhering to a single pattern in all situations is not optimum in most cases.

For example, if we compulsively avoid conflict, our needs remain unmet and our relationships suffer; we do not seem to care about ourselves, and we do not seem to care about others. When we always compete, we damage relationships and motivate reciprocal competitive behavior. If we compulsively seek compromise, we fail to discover creative approaches; we leave potential benefit on the table and force others to also surrender benefit. Habitual and unreasoned accommodation may result in a loss of self-respect and a surfeit of unsatisfied interests; unexpressed resentment may eventually cause stress or result in violence.

Note your habitual responses. The Thomas and Kilmann Conflict Mode Instrument is a tool that can help you explore and measure your habits. Once you score the test, read the descriptions of responses to conflict provided by Thomas and Kilmann.[2]

Our behavior within any single response category can be nuanced. We compete, compromise, or avoid in different ways. We may compete with charm or with brute force. For example, we may possess an affable style of competing that makes it difficult for others to recognize our unhealthy passion for winning; we may develop social graces that mask our intensity.

A study of your habitual responses will improve your ability to respond effectively. You can learn to pay attention to stimuli that trigger responses. You will want to observe how family, friends, and close associates draw you into conflict. Self-study can help you break habits and patterns that lead to failure.

Our purpose is not to reduce complex variables to simple answers, but rather to provoke observation of the unique and complex stream of thoughts, behaviors, emotions, and feelings that make up our world during a conflict.

✑

Using the chart, identify your most common response to conflict.

Have you fallen into a habitual pattern?

In this conflict, what were your original responses?

Were your responses reasoned or habitual and reactive?

How did your responses affect the conflict?

In this conflict, has the other party responded in a habitual and unreasoned manner?

SIX

Your Story

THE FIRST STEP in conflict resolution is preparing to tell your story—the story of what happened. In order to shape a better future, we must first unravel a troubled past. As we prepare to explain *what happened*, we gain insight into factors that led to conflict. In order to sharpen the focus of our account, we assess the exact nature of events that transpired. Our focus turns to fleshing out a narrative account.

THE CONFLICT NARRATIVE: WHAT HAPPENED?

Telling your story is vital. If you go to trial, your attorney will describe the dispute in legal briefs and oral arguments that help the judge or jury understand the dispute.[1] However, rules of evidence and trial procedure may force your attorney to present a story that does not reflect all aspects of reality. Ironically, a legal argument does not represent "the whole truth," and litigants commonly feel they did not have a chance to truly tell their story.

Mediation is different. It provides a forum in which you can tell your complete story. It allows you to explain your point of view, present your thoughts, and express your emotions and concerns.

❧

Will aspects of what happened in this dispute require more explanation than is possible in legal documents? Describe.

Will a mediation forum provide you with the opportunity to make sure you really have been heard?

CREATIVE USE OF NARRATIVE

The open-ended question "what happened" invites you to provide a narrative description of events — the story as told *from your point of view*. The mediator becomes an interested, active listener as you share the history of the conflict, from a personal, heartfelt viewpoint. When a mediator allows you to present your story *as you choose*, bias is avoided. Narrow questions, in contrast, tend to limit the narrative content, inadvertently shaping the story. For this reason, the mediator poses open-ended questions and listens to the story *as it is told*.

In most cultures, complex information is conveyed through story-telling. The story told in court, however, is shaped by the adversarial nature of the process. Mediation is different: its unedited narrative usually differs from the conflict narrative presented in legal briefs. Typically, it is only in this expanded mediation narrative that the actual conflict comes into focus. Thus, as you prepare for mediation, you will want to call upon emotions, perspectives, and meanings that allow you to best tell your story.

❧

What important aspects of your story might be overlooked?

Do you feel prepared to tell your story?

Will you need to improve the clarity of your narrative? How might you do that?

Will it help to have a friend play "detective" and pepper you with questions about your story?

THE HERO

We see ourselves as the hero in our own story — a beleaguered hero, but a hero nonetheless. Our story is shaped and formed by the traits of this heroic character. Decisions regarding possible solutions are fashioned within the framework of this character. A settlement outcome that does not match our inner narrative will not endure. Therefore, before we can accept a solution to a conflict, we must integrate the potential outcome into our personal story. The proposed future must be compatible with our hero's journey.

For example, if we perceive ourselves as virtuous heroes remedying a dangerous situation, we will not accept an outcome in which we are cast as a villain who wantonly caused harm. A resolution will not occur in the face of a story that contradicts our role as a heroic character.

On the other hand, we can accept a new narrative in which we are a well-intentioned character who acted on faulty information and accidentally caused harm for which we now apologize. In any event, the story that evolves must be consistent with our inner narrative — our view of "who we are."

Rarely will both parties tell an identical story. At the very least, they viewed events from different perspectives. After a while a party may decide that past differences are irrelevant to the future. They may cease arguing over which story shall be deemed "official truth." They may begin to take a genuine interest in the story the other party tells. They may realize that the other party's story is valid — for them.

Usually a party does not *really* know the person with whom they have become entangled in conflict. They do not truly know their adversary's *inner drama*, as they have never had an opportunity to listen closely to the other person's inner narrative.

When you realize that hope for peace lies in understanding the other party's motivations and interests, you listen at a deeper level. You may find it helps to consider that you are a detective and that the other party's story is a mystery from which you must extract vital clues that reveal a dramatic ending — reconciliation.

❦

What must the other party learn about you to better understand possible solutions?

What must you learn about the other party to better understand how to craft a resolution?

What do you imagine the other party wants to know about you?

What is there about the other party that makes you curious?

THE ROLE OF MYTH

Myth would seem to be the last thing we need when solving a dispute. However, we all imagine ourselves as heroic characters on a life journey, struggling with trials and tribulations that test our character.[2] Typically, we remain unaware of the subtle mythmaking that informs the inner life narrative. Only when we summon the script from our unconscious and explore our personal hero's journey do we begin to inquire into how the hero in our story addresses conflict.[3]

How does the hero in your life story handle conflict?

How do you typically overcome adversity?

Is this conflict an important episode in your life story or merely a distraction?

How will this dispute be integrated into your overall story?

CLARIFICATION

After posing open-ended questions, the mediator asks clarifying questions, following up on portions of the narrative that may not have been clear in the first telling. This is not a cross-examination you should fear, but rather a sign of the mediator's desire to understand. You are the expert on your dispute; the mediator needs your help to understand your situation.

The mediator then narrows the inquiry and poses close-ended questions often answered with "yes" or "no" or with factual information. Overall, the mediator's questions can be graphed as a funnel: broad open-ended questions narrow to a focus on details.[4] Try to be as transparent as possible, allowing the mediator to walk in your shoes and see the conflict through your eyes.

Do you become defensive when someone asks questions?

How will you help the mediator understand your story?

What do you feel might need the most explanation?

SEVEN

Assessing Conflict

A CONFLICT ASSESSMENT can enhance your narrative account and provide a deeper understanding of conflict drivers. As a result, your story becomes textured with insights that light up paths leading to resolution.

CONFLICT CAN BE UNDERSTOOD

Confusion and uncertainty surround conflict. Understanding feels just out of reach; the truth skirts past our comprehension. In order to restore clarity, we must first assess the underlying causes of conflict.

In addition, we must grasp the difference between a *problem* and a *conflict*. They are similar but not identical. Moving a large rock up a hill presents a problem but not a conflict, as gravity does not *intend* to oppose us. When we struggle with a conscious agent who *intends* to oppose us, we have conflict.

OPPOSING FORCES CREATE CONFLICT

Conflict arises from opposing or clashing goals, intentions, efforts, desires, interests, needs, values, beliefs, emotions, and identities.

Basic conflict dynamics include the following:

- We are prevented from having *something we want*.

- We are forced to accept *something we do not want*.

- We *pull toward us* things we desire, but they are withheld from us.

- We *push away things* that repulse us, but they are pushed on us.

- We *push or pull in opposition* to another.

- We *pull back* when someone tries to draw us toward them.

- We *push back* when someone pushes on us.

Identify clashing goals, intentions, efforts, and desires in your conflict.

Identify the push-and-pull dynamics of the conflict.

Who is trying to have something? Who opposes them?

Who rejects something? Who makes them accept what they reject?

Who is the conscious agent that opposes the outcome you desire or intend?

BE, DO, & HAVE

In your assessment consider:

1) *Who you want to be* that is opposed;

2) *What you want to do* that is opposed;

3) *What you want to have* that is opposed.

ASSESSING THE NEED TO HAVE

Conflict arises when we desire something and that desire is opposed. In our assessment, we identify who opposes us when we attempt to have possessions we need or want.

❧

What are you seeking to possess that is being withheld?

What desire, need, or intention to have is being opposed?

What property rights are in dispute?

MONEY

Money is a medium of exchange; it translates into the power to possess goods or services. The subject of money can become tainted with negative emotions from previous bad experiences. For this reason, you will want to assess past upsets regarding money, as those upsets influence your views on possessing things you need or want. Previous bad experiences may be a key factor in the current conflict.

Money derives its power from people's willingness to exchange symbols of value (paper money, metal coins or other financial instruments) for actual goods. When a symbol becomes complex, esoteric, or deceptive, conflict increases. During assessment you will want to identify any confusion regarding the means of exchange (money) that is driving the conflict.

❧

In this conflict, has there been confusion regarding money or other financial instruments?

Have negative emotions regarding money played a role in this conflict?

What values should guide the exchange of money or goods?

SCARCITY

Scarcity of goods means some people will have their needs met while others will be forced to go without. Moral rights and obligations come into play; fairness and justice may be debated. As a party to a conflict you will want to assess the degree to which scarcity, real or imagined, has been a factor in this dispute.

❧

What role does actual or imagined scarcity play in this dispute?

How might scarcity be remedied?

Must issues of fairness and justice with regard to property rights be resolved?

Has greed been involved? Describe.

EXPECTATIONS

Expectations — the ways we imagine or predict the future — factor into our continued survival. If we fail to correctly estimate our needs, our survival may be threatened. However, our expectations may turn into convictions regarding what we deserve. We assume our expectations will be met; we assume we will receive what we deserve. This assumption grows into an unshakeable expectation. When that expectation is disappointed, conflict flares. We feel intentionally wronged and seek to remedy our disappointment.

Unstated expectations can be especially troublesome. The cause of the conflict is hidden, as the *unstated expectation* exists only in the mind of a single party. For this reason, it is important to surface hidden or unstated expectations — our own and those of the other party.

❧

Are your expectations clearly stated?

Are your expectations realistic?

Do you know the other party's expectations?

Will expectations need to be modified?

Are agreements or contracts regarding possessions in dispute?

Do unmet expectations fuel the conflict?

ASSESSING THE NEED TO DO

Conflict emerges when *what we want to do* is opposed. When our behavior is stopped, restrained, or limited, particularly with coercive force, strife results. In this category we find abuse of power, domination, and coercion. Conflict may concern freedom of speech, freedom of movement, freedom to protest, freedom to pursue happiness, freedom to worship, or other freedoms to act as we choose.

Disputes emerge over accepted behavior; norms regulating permissible behavior are challenged; the question of who is allowed to set standards is debated. In cross-cultural settings, there is confusion regarding what constitutes disrespect.

How has your desire *to do* something or act in a certain way been opposed?

How have you opposed the other party's desire *to do* or act as they choose?

Has someone's freedom been constrained?

Does this conflict concern prohibited behavior?

What values prohibit or sanction the contested behavior?

In what way do you feel you have been unfairly stopped?

Has a behavior given offense?

Does someone seek to dominate or coerce another?

ASSESSING THE NEED TO BE

Opposition to *who we are* or *who we want to be* results in identity-based conflict. Position or title may be at stake. Our core identity—our view of our essential nature—may be under attack.

Conflict may concern who has the power to assign or impose identity—you may have heard the protest (frequently expressed by teenagers), "You don't get to tell me who I can be." Other examples include: "If that's who you want to be, you're not welcome here" or "We do not permit your kind here."

The following discussion briefly examines sources of identity conflict. As a party to a dispute, you will want to identify the factors that apply.

Status drives conflict when a desire for power or prestige is blunted. People who seek power or gain prestige often clash with those opposed to their ambitions.

Class distinctions erect boundaries that exclude those deemed inferior. In other cases, a person who fails to conform to an expected identity—in a family, a business, a group, or a community—risks becoming an outcast. Exclusion from a group breeds discontent that later morphs into overt hostility. Many conflicts are driven by a sense of exclusion.

In a similar manner, *group identity* (deriving one's identity from membership in a group) generates conflict: being a member of one group may automatically make you the enemy of a rival group. *Ethnic feuds* frequently drive violence; strong collective identity may lead to "us versus them" thinking.

Identity may be based on external characteristics or on circumstances of birth. While we can modify our desire for possessions and while we can restrain our behavior, *physical identity* is less flexible. Thus, prejudice based on physical characteristics can be particularly cruel and can lead to heated conflict. This is one reason society enacts hate crimes legislation.

Identity includes inner qualities — *personality* traits, *beliefs*, or *preferences* — based largely on personal choices that determine our unique character. When our freedom to express this uniqueness is challenged, conflict emerges. The importance of maintaining a distinct individual identity varies among cultures: some cultures place importance on individual expression or even eccentricity, while others mandate conformity.

There are many ways in which identity — our desire *to be* — gives rise to conflict. You will want to assess the role this plays in your particular dispute.

&

How does this conflict impinge on who you would like *to be*?

Does the other party seek to restrict your identity?

Do you feel you have been persecuted as a result of your identity?

Is one party seeking to "make nothing" of the other?

Does this conflict concern "us versus them" group dynamics?

How important will it be for you to defend your group?

Has someone been insulted?

Is status, prestige, position, title, or power at stake?

Is pride a factor?

Has another attacked an aspect of your core identity such as your faith, beliefs, or values?

Is there a need to restrain a harmful identity? Describe.

THE NEED TO BE RIGHT

A special case of the need *to be* is the need *to be right*. The emotions generated when this need is blunted can be extremely strong: *being right* becomes equivalent to survival; *being wrong* becomes associated with non-survival.

Imagine you are driving on a mountain road that has been washed out. If you continue, you will plummet off a cliff. If you correctly anticipate the distance to the cliff edge, you will be able to apply the brakes in time and avoid catastrophe. If you miscalculate the distance, you will catapult to your death.

Building on such experience, the unconscious mind comes to equate *being right* with survival and *being wrong* with non-survival. In most instances, survival is a matter of degree. Choices we make allow us to survive and prosper, or they diminish our survival and prosperity.

As a result, when someone "makes us wrong," we experience a surprising overreaction: intuition signals that our survival is threatened. We habitually defend our rightness as though our lives depend on it—even when the stakes are insignificant. Thus, even when life-and-death outcomes are *not* at stake, strong emotions accompany being right and wrong. Conflict takes on exaggerated importance and urgency. Telling someone they are wrong provokes strong emotions—even if done tactfully. The "I'm right and you're wrong" dynamic is *extremely* powerful and should not be overlooked.

✋

In this conflict, has someone insisted you were wrong?

Have you experienced a difficult time convincing the other party you were right?

Have you felt your survival is under attack? Is it possible you have overreacted?

Has the other party defended himself as though his life were on the line?

In what way might you diminish the threat you pose to the other party?

Is it possible to assure the other party they were right about something?

Must the other party admit you were right before resolution is possible?

BE, DO, HAVE INTERDEPENDENCE

We have considered *being*, *doing*, and *having* individually — in practice they are interdependent. Typically, we act (*do*) in order to own (*have*) things that support our identity (*be*). As you map your dispute, assess how these factors are related. If negotiation hangs up, it may signal that too much importance has been given one factor to the exclusion of others.

◈

What do you need *to do* in order *to have* what you want?

Or what do you need *to be* in order *to do* what we want?

Or what must you *have* in order *to be* who you want to be?

Assess the relations between your needs and desires.

Describe what you were trying to *be*, *do*, and *have* in this conflict.

Is it possible that you or the other party misread what is important or unimportant in this conflict?

FEELINGS ARE IMPORTANT

Assessment is not restricted to logic or intellect. All stories have an emotional arc. If you fail to understand the role emotions play in a conflict, you will not truly understand the conflict. For example, when you are prevented from possessing something you want, you experience a visceral reaction—jealousy, frustration, longing, or grief. The emotional response becomes part of your narrative. When you are stopped from acting (doing) as you wish, you feel enslaved, hurt, fearful, frustrated, or enraged.

Nowhere are feelings more important than in identity-based conflict. When you are denied possessions, you can give an account of your loss; when your freedom to act has been frustrated, you can decry being stopped, restrained, or imprisoned. But when it comes to your identity, feelings become the heart of your story. Identity is so intimately tied to emotions—I *am* sad, I *am* angry—that we often name our state of being with an emotion or feeling.

During this conflict, what emotions or feelings have been the strongest?

Have you been able to effectively communicate your feelings?

Will a "feelings conversation" need to be part of mediation?

Are there emotions that will be difficult for you to express?

PERSONAL HISTORICAL WOUNDS

Past trauma may drive conflict, as historical wounds become part of who we are and determine how likely we are to be drawn into conflict.

Repeated emotional trauma motivates us to build defensive walls. Subsequently, a violation of our protected emotional space, even if accidental and unintentional, may be perceived as a threat. When painful memories are triggered, our past hops into the driver's seat. Hair-trigger sensitivity to stimuli warns us that an enemy is present — though the enemy exists only in our past. We tend to fight yesterday's battles.

Psychological defenses become early warning devices that sound an alarm, sometimes causing us to initiate conflict prematurely. When current events mirror past upsets, we initiate an "offense is the best defense" strategy. The simplest provocation activates contentious tactics; as a result, we appear overly sensitive, easy to offend, edgy, irritable, and unpredictable.

At an unconscious level, we may be fighting a villain from our past at whose hands we suffered, rather than the person presently in front of us. We must evaluate our responses cautiously — does a present danger really exist? Likewise, we must ask, is the other party fighting an enemy from their past?

Nonetheless, do not overlook actual coercion, abuse of power, and present attempts to do harm. At times your defenses work *for you* rather than against you — you might be in actual danger. The challenge is discerning whether or not a real and present danger exists. A well-prepared narrative is one tool that can aid you during such discernment.

In rare instances, one party intends the destruction of the other, as a result of unbridled narcissism or evil intention. However, too often we err in ascribing evil to another; we tend to demonize those with whom we disagree. Less frequently we commit the opposite error — we fail to recognize actual evil. An honest and thorough assessment helps us avoid falsely attributing evil or failing to recognize actual evil.

⚘

In what ways does this conflict resemble other conflicts you have experienced in the past?

In what ways does this conflict differ from previous conflicts?

Are long-term emotional challenges a part of this conflict?

Does the other party remind you of someone else you once knew? Describe.

Will you need to resolve earlier conflicts before attempting to resolve this one?

Has the other party confused you with someone else?

Has this conflict opened old wounds?

Is someone out to harm you? Describe.

PROCEDURAL FLAWS

Communication failures, poorly crafted contracts, accidents and unforeseen "acts of God," as well as other missteps, fuel disputes. Confusing communications distort events, generating conflict. Likewise, faulty procedures that hamper performance cause frustration. When cumbersome or misguided procedures are enforced, it seems people are intentionally erecting roadblocks, even though such impediments may simply be the result of poor planning, inefficient systems, and flawed organization. These institutional flaws, which can be resolved quickly, may be overlooked, leading disputants to blame individuals.

Bureaucratic and administrative roadblocks, however, may be covert tools that disgruntled or destructive employees employ for sabotage. When a procedural problem does not resolve, it may be masking a more serious personnel problem. A disgruntled employee may be using administrative errors and procedural barriers as smokescreens to hide their covert opposition. Proper assessment sheds light on the real situation.

❦

What role do procedural problems play in this conflict?

Has anything regarding procedures been unclear?

Is this conflict the result of omitted, incomplete, or misleading communication?

Has something been misunderstood?

Has frustration with the way things are organized caused conflict?

What rules are standing in your way?

Is this conflict simply a misunderstanding?

CONFLICT ESCALATION PATTERNS

Conflicts escalate in predictable patterns.[1] If you identify the current stage of escalation, you can predict the future path of the conflict and begin to control events. Unfortunately, you may hesitate to act until dire consequences force your hand. If a dispute is not sufficiently ripe — if you or the other party do not anticipate suffering adverse consequences — then convening will be difficult. False hope may lead you or the other party to believe the conflict might simply disappear without action on your part.

The escalation pattern is predictable. Friedrich Glasl described the steps:[2]

- You have lost faith in resolving the matter through fair discussions.

- Talking is useless; it is time to act unilaterally. The other party also feels talking is useless.

- You have used deniable punishment. The other party has used deniable punishment.[3]

- Veiled attacks have been made.

- Your honor has been offended. You have offended the other party's honor.

- Actions have taken place that would cause another to lose face.

- Threats and ultimatums have been issued.

- It is time to stop the other side from controlling you.

- It is time to attack the other party and destroy their ability to operate.

- You no longer care if you survive; your greatest wish is to destroy the other party.

These steps can be reduced to the following descriptive stages:[4]

Stage 1. Hardening

Stage 2. Debate & Polemics

Stage 3. Actions, Not Words

Stage 4. Images & Coalitions

Stage 5. Loss of Face

Stage 6. Strategies of Threat

Stage 7. Limited Destructive Blows

Stage 8. Fragmentation of the Enemy

Stage 9. Together into the Abyss

You can avoid escalation to the next higher stage. You can change direction and purposely de-escalate the conflict, perhaps offering concessions that signal your good intentions, making it easier for the other party to consider mediation.

❦

What stage of escalation has been reached?

Where is this fight headed?

What do you fear might happen?

What can be done to wind down conflict?

THE IMPORTANCE OF ASSESSMENT

Thoughtful analysis prepares you to convey what happened; it helps you uncover factors that need to be addressed if conflict is to be resolved. Assessment brings to light the negative consequences of leaving conflict unresolved. Your success in mediation will be determined in great measure by how diligent you are in your assessment.

Will you need help completing your assessment?

What other factors will you need to assess?

How might your preparation affect the other party?

Will a thorough understanding of the conflict allow you to proceed with greater confidence?

EIGHT

Faulty Perceptions

OUR PERCEPTIONS ARE colored by emotions, values, biases, history, and prejudices. They are not always accurate. This does not mean our perceptions lack all veracity: there is always some truth in our account of events, as the way we perceive the other is real *for us*. Thus, in mediation we do not completely disregard our suspicions, but we also do not allow our negative view of the other to become rigid. Our views must remain subject to revision.

During mediation, you test your perceptions at the same time you listen closely to discover how the other party perceives you. Discovering what character you play in their "movie" allows you to renegotiate your role. Initially, it can be startling to discover how your adversary sees you — the character you play in their drama is not who you know yourself to be. You have been misperceived, just as you may have miscast the other party. In mediation, the negotiation of identity begins in earnest. As you rewrite your narrative, you help the other party rewrite and polish their script.

This does not mean you will end up perceiving the other party exactly as they perceive themselves. A perfect match may be impossible. Nonetheless, each party realizes the other is *not as bad as I originally thought*. You renegotiate your relationship and recast your roles. As you share your respective inner narratives — the "why" behind your actions — perceptions are adjusted. When you hear the other person describe motivations driving their actions, you may see how what they did makes sense from *their* viewpoint. Also, when you discover you have been misrepresented and misunderstood, you are motivated to tell your story to set the record straight. You evaluate less-than-accurate views, eliminate errors, and recalibrate perceptions.

❧

Are you prepared to listen to a different version of events?

How important will it be for you to explain events in your own words?

How important will it be for you to hear the other party explain what they did in their own words?

TAINTED PERCEPTIONS

As you prepare your narrative, you typically draft a description of the villain who opposes you. This portrait may play well in your version of the story, but in mediation you must verify its accuracy. You must perform a reality check in which you unearth bias or error.

As you look back at prior conflicts, you may recall hurting another as a result of a rush-to-judgment that led you to act unwisely or unfairly. You may have assumed the other party harbored evil motives, which prompted you to take punitive action; only later did you discover your error. Thus, we often live with uncertainty, wondering if our actions were justified. Reflecting on past errors will help you recognize just how easily faulty perceptions can fuel conflict.

To remedy the bias or error, you will want to listen to the other party's story. When we cling to misperceptions, the conciliation process comes to a standstill. Listening to your adversary's narrative, however, provides you with a reality check. You can play detective and seek supporting evidence for your hunches. At this early stage you may concentrate not so much on changing your perceptions but rather on simply identifying them. You need to get a fix on exactly how you see the world.

❧

Have you had the experience of unfairly judging another only to later find out you were wrong?

How will you make sure you are not operating on false impressions?

How will you identify your biases and prejudices?

FALSE ATTRIBUTIONS

We typically interpret the behavior of others by making assumptions regarding their motives. We imagine their inner narrative; we craft a story that explains *why* they acted as they did. We construct a story that makes sense, ascribing motive and intention to our antagonist. We imagine a stream of consciousness, an inner narrative that explains *their* behavior in a way that makes our story hang together.

When we assign causes, we select from two categories: *dispositional* causes such as character, attitudes, intentions, and *situational* causes in which behavior is motivated by external circumstances. We attribute the behavior of others to dispositional factors, while we attribute our own behavior to situational factors. This brings about bias called *false attribution error* in which we incorrectly attribute motive or disposition to another.[1]

We excuse our own behavior, attributing cause to external circumstances beyond our control (situational causes). At the same time, we attribute the other person's behavior to bad character or evil motives (dispositional causes). We grant ourselves the benefit of a doubt based on intimate knowledge of our subjective reality; but we see the other party's behavior arising from evil motive or flawed character.

Stereotypes contribute to such false attribution. When we script the other party's inner story—their disposition, character, and intention—stereotypes seep in. Partial truths bolster the story we draft.

Unfortunately, we often do not recognize the assumptions written into our inner narratives. We assume our perceptions align with reality "out there." In fact, our biases alter our view of reality. To correct this alteration, we must work to include the other person's actual inner narrative in our view of reality. We must engage in the hard work of overcoming false attributions — but such on-the-fly assumptions settle into our consciousness and are hard to remove.

When parties express contradictory accounts, mediators know both cannot be factual. Yet each account is true *for the individual*. The mediator does not adjudicate which reality is true but rather acknowledges the truth in both accounts. Then she helps disputants co-author a future narrative.

But rewriting is difficult. Once assigned, imagined character flaws and evil intentions become difficult to erase. We unconsciously search for evidence to verify the story we created, cobbling together supporting details that make our story work. In order to reverse this error, we need to view the opposing party as a mystery to be solved rather than as a cardboard character to be propped up.

⸎

Have you ascribed evil intentions or evil motives to the other party? Describe.

What did you observe that led to such assumptions?

How would you describe the other party's character flaws?

Has the other party attributed evil intentions to you?

What might have caused the attribution of evil to you?

How might the other party describe your character flaws?

OVERCOMING FALSE ATTRIBUTIONS

In some cases, we attribute evil intentions when they do not exist; in other cases, we assume evil intentions do not exist, when in fact they do. In the former instance, we err by erecting an arbitrary barrier; in the latter, we err by blithely opening the door for those who intend harm.

Thus, you face the dichotomy between relationship-destroying paranoia and self-destructive glibness; you vacillate between unwarranted fear and hopeful naïveté. The challenge is avoiding the error of demonizing the other party by mistake, while not failing to unmask a genuine demon, should one exist. To accomplish this task, approach the other party with healthy skepticism, as a mystery to be solved; embrace healthy curiosity and a sense of discovery. Be open to unexpected revelations.

Mediation will help you differentiate actual evil intentions from false attributions. You will revisit and re-examine events; you will work through varying accounts of what happened; you will share explanations and gather information that dispels falsehoods. Your adversary will fill in the blanks in your story; in turn, you fill in the blanks in their narrative. You acquire material needed to rewrite your master narrative and you provide answers the other party needs to reconstruct their narrative. Initially you may be reticent to share motives, intentions, and feelings, but eventually you will come to understand the importance of co-authoring a new narrative.

⤙⤚

List possible alternative reasons for the other party's behavior.

Recall instances when you behaved like the other party.
Describe your motives and intentions at those times.

How might you clarify the intentions of the other party?

What do you need to make clear so the other party understands your intentions?

SUBJECTIVITY

Our world is colored by emotions. Some consider emotions in a negative light: emotions foil our rational intentions. In mediation, however, we

61

do not eschew emotional subjectivity; rather, we seek to correct emotional distortions. We acknowledge emotions as valuable when they are appropriate to the situation.

As the authors of *Difficult Conversations* note, "Each side must have their feelings *acknowledged*... Acknowledgment is a step that simply cannot be skipped."[2] When we acknowledge feelings, we ratify that which is most real for the other party, since feelings are inextricably linked to that other party's perception of reality. Acknowledgment, however, does not mean we *agree* with their reality. Rather we *recognize* what constitutes reality *for them*. We let them know we sincerely want to know how they see the world.

⤸

What must you do to acknowledge the other party's feelings?

Does the other party feel you understand them?

Do you feel the other party understands you?

What is the biggest disagreement with the other party regarding what is real?

DESTRUCTIVE EMOTIONS

The most ubiquitous destructive emotion, which is fear, can protect us from adverse consequences. Fear can serve as a valid warning. However, fear often sends us down paths of self-destruction and often motivates us to harm others.

During mediation, we are asked to sit with our fears. We are asked to put our fears on hold even though it causes discomfort. In mediation, rather than avoid our fears, we use them as a window on the conflict.

Fear usually signals the presence of adverse consequences that we must avoid or overcome. It triggers a flight-or-fight response. Thus, during a mediation assessment we will want to explore the adverse consequences that trigger our fear. We ponder the consequences our opponent will inflict on us if we do not accede to their demands. What harm will they make us suffer? What will they take from us? What unwanted conditions will they force us to experience?

Exploring consequences can clarify your vision of the other person. Your fears define your antagonist: he or she is the character who will render you bankrupt, take your job, gain custody of your children, or cause you physical or emotional pain.

Two additional destructive emotions are anger and rage. With fear, we anticipate consequences we will suffer at the hands of another; with anger and rage, we anticipate adverse consequences we intend to exact. Fear speaks to how we will be harmed; anger and rage speak to how we will deliver harm.

Anger and rage are common in conflict, the result of opposing forces locked in place. You cannot or will not turn away; the other party cannot or will not turn away. This oppositional embrace generates a need-to-destroy that manifests as anger and rage. From an emotional distance you would recognize other options, other ways to satisfy your needs. But when you cannot distance yourself from the conflict, you feel trapped and that feeling turns to rage. In extreme cases, destruction of the other party begins to take precedence over your survival.

✦

Have you experienced fear in this dispute? Describe.

Has the other party been afraid of you? Describe.

Have you given in to anger or rage in this conflict?

Have you been confronted with the anger or rage of the other party?

What about this conflict triggers emotional distress?

How do you keep destructive emotions under control?

What process guidelines will be necessary to keep destructive emotions under control?

Will emotional catharsis — the positive release of emotion — be necessary?

How easy is it for you to express distressing emotions? Will you need help?

NEGATIVE EMOTIONS HAMPER RECONCILIATION

Destructive emotions motivate *wall building*. Walls protect us when we are afraid and restrain us when we feel rage. Walls protect us from others and protect others from us. When an actual threat exists, being without walls can be dangerous. Building walls that trap us within is also dangerous, leaving us secluded and disconnected. Others must destroy walls to reach us; we must destroy walls to reach them. Walls become impediments to reconciling relationships; they enforce separation.

When we are cut off, we feel an urge to knock down the other party's walls; we want them to see us and hear us; we want them to know we exist and have needs; we want them to know we suffer. When our needs are frustrated, the defenses erected by another become an affront that provokes our attack — the very outcome the wall was constructed to prevent.

A mediation approach calls for balance: we leave in place walls needed for safety and we destroy walls that serve no purpose. Mediators facilitate the transformation of walls into bridges. Parties are not completely exposed; rather, during collaboration they identify and remove the specific walls that are blocking resolution.

Mediation guidelines maintain safety while you draw closer to the other party. Process guidelines and measured steps ensure your physical and emotional safety.

How will you manage your fears so they do not hamper your ability to resolve the conflict?

How will you address the other party's fears?

Sketch a picture of the walls you put in place to protect you in this conflict.

Now add walls the other uses to protect themselves.

What walls will need come down in order for resolution to take place?

Where might you begin building a bridge?

Write a short character sketch describing your opponent in this conflict. Label the description "tentative" or "rough draft."

NINE

Communication

COMMUNICATION BARRIERS FREQUENTLY block mediation success. If you cannot communicate with the other party, resolution is unlikely.

For example, assume someone has a hostile attitude toward you. Now assume it is based on false information. In an effort to correct the misinformation, you ask, "What happened to make you think *that*?" The other party, however, views your attempt to clarify the misunderstanding as an attack and assumes a defensive posture: "I don't have to justify myself to you." You take their rejection to heart and become equally defensive.

In a similar fashion, if you suggest a solution, your suggestion may be seen as a strategic move intended to benefit only you. The other party fears hidden motives. While your solution may be valid, it is rejected simply because *you* originated it. The other party devalues your ideas and responds negatively solely because you are the opposition.

When parties attempt to resolve a conflict on their own, the natural dynamics of conflict create impasse. The disputants are trapped in patterns they cannot change without the help of an impartial third party.

Similar dynamics occur when you consider sharing candid feelings: you crash headlong into a wall of anxiety. Exposing your inner self not only feels unsafe, it may *be* unsafe. Your physical and emotional reactions stop you in your tracks. Anxiety and stress send the message, "Don't expose yourself. Don't become vulnerable." You may want to share honest feelings, but you also want to avoid emotional injury. One defensive posture triggers another and creates the dichotomy: "I must express myself—but I can't express myself."

In addition, difficult emotions blur perceptions and make communication difficult. We secretly wonder: "Am I seeing things as they really are? Dare I say anything?" Eventually we fend off uncertainty by adopting the frame of mind: "there is only one reality—mine." When doubt and uncertainty swell, we either become confused or we become rigid with tunnel vision, unable to enter into dialogue to explore other viewpoints.

A mediator changes the dynamics. He does not stand in opposition to either party and does not play the role of an authority figure. He has no stake in the outcome, nothing to gain. He provides each party with a safe person to whom they can express vulnerable feelings.

✤

Will a mediator need to facilitate communication?

What will you need to share with the mediator about your previous communication with the other party?

In the past, did you and the other party experience good communication?

What, if anything, happened to impair your communication?

HUMILITY RATHER THAN JUDGMENT

Communication flows through many sense channels conveying complex states of mind. A mediator listens to spoken and written words, to body language, including eye contact, to actions conveying intention and meaning, to heart messages and intuition.

The last thing a party wants is judgment, but paradoxically, they do not desire coddling sympathy. They seek empathy—understanding without judgment. They eschew sympathy designed to make them feel good no matter the nature of their transgressions; they seek someone who can hear the good and the bad and separate their actions from their identity and allow them to create a better future. We all love an uncritical ally, but we also value someone who can reflect the truth of who we are in our many colors, including our shadows. But we also hope we will feel better about who we are after we reconcile.

It is worth noting that a mediator is not a therapist, and yet mediation may be therapeutic. A therapist evaluates and makes judgments, often labeling the parties, overtly or covertly. In contrast, a mediator does not label or diagnose; instead, she facilitates a self-determined journey toward reconciliation.

❦

What type of mediator assistance will be most helpful?

How will you help the mediator foster an honest and candid conversation?

ACTIVE LISTENING

Empathetic listening may also be called *active listening*. A mediator seeks to put himself in your shoes. He paraphrases and asks if he has understood you correctly. As he has no stake in the outcome, his examination of the narrative is non-threatening.

A mediator may revisit the narrative, soliciting different points of view; this might include having you recount events with selective focus on different senses. He may ask for an account of what you saw, followed by what you heard, and then he might ask how events may have appeared from the other party's vantage point.

A mediator frames narratives using non-threatening neutral language. As much as possible, he avoids emotional triggers that lead to defensive posturing. As he is not part of the upset, he is not subject to destructive emotions. Thus he can provide parties with an opportunity to tell their stories without triggering destructive emotional feedback. He does not ignore emotional content but rather paraphrases with a neutral perspective that diminishes emotional triggering.

❧

Do you feel comfortable working with a mediator on strategies for resolution?

What help do you feel would be most valuable?

Do you find it easy to express "matters of the heart"?

Will you need to find better ways of expressing your concerns?

LISTENING TO SELF

It is valuable to listen to the signals your words and emotions send. At the same time you tell your story, you engage in deep listening. Listen to your heart—there may be more to the story than was apparent at the outset.

Uncovering deeper aspects of conflict may require spending time in a quiet place or taking long walks that encourage reflection. We need to observe our thoughts and emotions as a stranger might observe them, from a distance. We allow ourselves to be surprised by new insights. We watch our thoughts and emotions flow past from a detached vantage point on the banks of our stream of consciousness. We seek to become more perceptive and better able to hear our heart's messages.

❧

Will it be advantageous for you to spend quiet time contemplating your situation?

How do you usually get in touch with your heartfelt emotions?

What must you do to become a calm observer of this conflict?

How might you remove barriers that prevent calm introspection?

FRAMING

There are many ways to convey concerns: some increase understanding and willingness to collaborate; others trigger negative emotions and destroy willingness to communicate. A mediator models good framing skills, presenting information in ways the parties can hear.

A mediator helps a party avoid triggering unwanted emotions in their opponent. He helps a party tell the same story with a different frame. One valuable frame involves using *I messages* that speak in first-person terms, explaining how events made us feel rather than saying "this is what you did to me."[1]

Avoiding all negative reactions is impossible; rather, the effort is to minimize negative emotions so as to build dialogue momentum. A mediator helps parties find language conducive to reconciliation, language that draws parties together rather than pushing them apart.

∾

Will you need assistance in finding better ways to frame your communication?

Has a previous communication brought about a hardening of positions?

AVOID BLAMING

Framing helps avoid "I am right and you are wrong" dichotomies; framing avoids blaming. While you have a need to be right, you do not need to make the other person wrong. You may assume that if you make yourself right, the other party must be wrong, but this is not always the case. You can narrate events without commentary that assigns blame. Multiple perspectives can co-exist in a dynamic network of views rather than being framed as polar opposites.

When we engage in deeper discussion, we avoid a rush to assign blame. A matter-of-fact dialogue can avoid acrimony and unproductive positioning. It avoids communication peppered with "you did this to me" allegations. This does not mean you will avoid discussing how the other's actions affected you; rather, you let your hurt be known in a frame that focuses on your pain — not on blame.

Faced with blame, we become reticent to continue the conflict resolution process; we may be willing to attempt reconciliation, but we are not about to submit to blame, particularly at the outset. One solution is "I messages."

❦

Do you fear you will be called on to admit failings? How does that make you feel?

Do you hope the other party will admit they were wrong?

How important is it that you be acknowledged for having been right?

Is there a way to resolve this conflict without affixing appropriate blame?

USING "I MESSAGES"

At first glance, you might argue that such an approach is simply avoidance. Why not just tell the truth? "You hurt me. That is what happened." While this view has merit, it lacks pragmatic value. When you accuse, you risk ending the conversation. Few people tolerate being made wrong; most people will shut down and walk away.

If you state that you felt harmed, however, it is difficult for the other to challenge you — that is what *you felt* and only you know how *you felt*. The other party may claim they would have felt different — but that does not address how you felt.

When you use "I messages" to speak of your hurt, the door opens for the other party to enter the narrative, as they are not triggered into a defensive posture. They may even express empathy and acknowledge they caused injury, while explaining their intention was not to cause pain. They may apologize, accept responsibility, and express remorse. In contrast, the likely response to blame is an angry self-defense. We experience blame as an attack on our identity. We are more likely to offer an apology and make amends when we are *not* under attack.

❦

Prior to mediation, spend time practicing "I messages."

Evaluate the changes in others that "I messages" bring about.

CATHARSIS

At the beginning of mediation, parties hesitate to unleash negative emotions, fearing the discomfort. They decline to engage honestly, tacitly agreeing to keep feelings bottled up. They skirt difficult emotions and try to move directly to problem solving. Unexpressed emotions, however, may later stall the process. Parties cannot view each other accurately through their unsettled emotions; distortion is inevitable. False attributions emerge.

A double bind ensues: absent emotional release, parties will not move forward, yet they fear such release will be unpleasant. For this reason, we seek to vent pent-up emotions in a controlled manner. We seek creative ways of purging anger, rage, jealousy, and fear. We seek catharsis — the cleansing of troublesome emotion. We want to transform negative emotions into bridge-building materials. Often this takes place in private sessions with the mediator during which a party may unearth, purge, and transform negative emotions.

Once again, it is important to note that mediation is *not* therapy, yet it *is* therapeutic. In our culture, we tend to sequester emotional discourse as though it were a pathology to be addressed exclusively by a mental health professional. Emotions that emerge in conflict resolution, however, are not signs of pathology but rather a natural, healthy component of life.

The authors of *Difficult Conversations* note, "The problem is that when feelings are at the heart of what's going on, they are the business at hand and ignoring them is nearly impossible."[2] Destructive emotions will be present — it is part of the conflict landscape.

When you manage emotions, you see others in a profoundly more accurate light. When you release fear, anger, rage, and self-pity, you enjoy greater success. The tendency to demonize the other with false attributions gives way to empathy that inspires understanding of your opponent's inner narrative.

⚶

Do you find it difficult to experience emotion?

What challenges do you anticipate when it comes to difficult emotions?

How might the mediator assist you when it comes to emotions?

In this conflict, have emotions been suppressed?

In this conflict, have emotions been rejected?

In this conflict, has anyone been made wrong for feelings?

What emotional events will need to be discussed?

TEN

Discovery

IN BOTH LITIGATION and mediation, evidence is compiled and shared in a process known as *discovery*. In mediation, discovery is less formal and might be called "finding out what happened." This differs from litigation discovery, a formal procedure guided by rules of evidence and judicial rulings on pre-trial motions. The rules and decisions from the bench often determine which evidence is admissible and how it may be presented.

Early in litigation, a legal brief presented to the court explains the reason the party (plaintiff or petitioner) filed a suit. The document lays out the complaint and petitions the court for remedies, offering legal reasons the party is entitled to relief the court can grant. The opposing party (defendant or respondent) may submit a response, explaining why the suit (complaint) is inappropriate, invalid, or lacking in merit.

These legal briefs contain statements of fact a party believes are relevant and true, along with a discussion of applicable law. Motions determining which evidence may be presented are argued. Gathering the underlying evidence can be grueling. Attorneys often summon the opposing party for face-to-face questioning called a deposition. Questions are posed and responses are recorded, frequently on videotape. Later, at trial, written excerpts may be read or the video may be screened. Attorneys also may compel the production of documents or other evidence.

Discovery begins an adversarial contest in which parties attempt to discredit each other. Trial lawyers seek to impeach the testimony of the opposing party and destroy their credibility. Discovery, it may be assumed, unmasks a deceptive party and vindicates an honest party.

However, the evidence may not reflect the actual lived experience driving the conflict. Furthermore, the process may incite additional hostility, which lessens subsequent willingness to enter into good-faith negotiations.

In rare instances, discovery may inadvertently create a willingness to mediate. When a party faces testifying under oath and incurring possible penalties for deception, or when they fear being unmasked before a jury, they may entertain the thought of engaging in conflict resolution. In most cases, however, adversarial discovery causes the opposite response—positions harden. Parties resort to hair-splitting and half-truths. The result is a shallow truth that lacks the richness of freely given exposition regarding what happened.

The adversarial process may create harsh feelings that later inhibit mediation. Hostility may stifle willingness to engage in a candid discussion. Face may be seriously damaged; relationships destroyed; positions hardened. Emotional residue from overly aggressive discovery in which the party's integrity was attacked taints conflict resolution discussions.

There are exceptions. There are times when a deposition may convince a stubborn party their position is not as strong as they once thought. They may realize that under harsh cross-examination they will falter and fail to impress a jury. This realization may motivate them to mediate rather than engage in a courtroom contest. When an opposing party refuses to mediate, there may be value in providing the "reality check" of aggressive discovery, but more often than not the tactic turns a willing party into a hostile party.

❧

Will you mediate before litigation discovery takes place? Why or why not?

Has discovery created hostility that inhibits willingness to mediate?

If so, how will you remedy the problem?

What are you hoping to achieve in discovery?

What facts will be contested?

Are those facts critical for a negotiated settlement?

MEDIATION CHANGES THE GAME

In mediation, you want to seek to understand the other party rather than impugn their credibility. You want clarity. You seek candor, honesty and give-and-take disclosure. Your approach changes from "prove it" to "help me understand." The past is relevant only to the degree it helps you negotiate the future; the result you seek is not a verdict but rather an agreement.

If past events require clarification (or apologies and amends), those events are taken up, but they are not explored in order to assign blame and target punishment. They are taken up to clarify precipitating causes and ensure that harmful actions are not repeated.

You may remedy imbalances, injustices, or inequities that, if left unaddressed, will continue to generate conflict. You do not ignore the past but rather place a forward-looking frame around events that transpired.

Mediation thus alters the focus of discovery; facts go beyond those sought in litigation. In a trial, complex and subtle emotions are rendered irrelevant, whereas, in mediation, revealing emotional factors is vital. Mediators engage in a much finer-grained exploration of motivation and perspective, sharing information or feelings previously hidden. We reveal fears and personal concerns, including heartfelt expressions of apology and regret, which are out of place in a trial.

As the focus shifts, stories become more authentic; fuzzy black-and-white television becomes pristine high-definition. In litigation, parties defend false selves in a courtroom drama; in mediation, parties present a more honest self—a flawed self who hurts, suffers, cares, loves, hates, transgresses, and falls short.

In a trial, parties hide shortcomings, as their flaws are the weapons the other side uses to destroy them. In mediation, shortcomings are revealed as we express our intention to make up for past damage. In court, we defiantly seek to be exonerated or deemed victorious; in mediation, we acknowledge a flawed past and create a better future.

Confidentiality statutes make candid discussion possible. If additional privacy is important, you may want to negotiate additional confidentiality provisions. In addition, you may wish to agree on how the results of mediation will be made known upon settlement. Sometimes a public statement is appropriate while at other times the outcome should remain private.

What role will confidentiality statutes play?

Will you need additional confidentiality provisions?

What concerns do you have regarding confidentiality?

What information will you disclose in order for the other party to become fully informed?

What information will you need to obtain from the other party?

Do you suspect that information has been omitted or hidden by the other party?

Have you hidden or omitted vital information?

What facts do you believe will be contested?

On which facts will you and the other party agree?

PRESENTING "WHAT HAPPENED"

You may assume you understand the other party's motives, but upon hearing their firsthand account you may see events in an unexpected light. Differences in perspective will never be erased entirely, as facts exist within a subjective context. However, mediation embraces this flexible reality and accommodates mutually exclusive reality claims. The malleable nature of reality provides freedom for us to structure a new reality that encompasses the needs of multiple parties.

Once, I commented to participants, "You're in the same theater, but you're watching different movies." Subjective interpretations produced different versions of the conflict. In such situations, your goal is not to tell the best story (to convince a judge to render a verdict in your favor) but rather to tell the story that best reflects your personal experience.

As a result, you begin to accept the other party's version *as their experience*. You may respond, "That's not the way I saw it happen. But I'll agree that is *how you experienced it*." Often, they reciprocate, agreeing that your version is how you experienced events.

$\approx$

How will it help for both parties to have all the facts?

Will you be able to accept the idea that the other party may have seen reality in a different manner?

ELEVEN

Managing Deception

YOU MAY PROTEST: "Hold on. Doesn't a trial determine the truth? Don't we need a process that identifies who is lying and who is not? Doesn't litigation discovery ensure no one will benefit from a lie?" In fact, there is no such guarantee; frequently a lie prevails.

There are times, in a court setting, when detection and punishment of deception becomes the primary goal, times when unmasking a lie is appropriate. But usually you are more concerned with satisfying your interests than with exposing lies. You prefer meeting your long-term needs. Though it may seem counterintuitive, focusing on lie detection may diminish your ability to satisfy your interests.

Exposing deception in a judicial setting involves correctly identifying lies, but often leads to ambiguous results. At times we are dealing with willful attempts to deceive, but most of the time we simply encounter differing subjective truths. When deception is unambiguous, a verdict may punish the deceiver; more often, however, a verdict must overlook subtle differing subjective truths.

A jury views a blurry picture in which truth and fabrication are interwoven. As a result, they may reward the half-truth that is presented most convincingly. The pressure to find for one party rather than another may lead to the dismissal of perfectly honest testimony. This is especially true when partial truths exist on both sides.

It is common for frustrated juries to conclude that both parties are untruthful. Nonetheless, they must render a verdict. Given an opportunity to express their frank assessment, they might instruct both parties to consult their consciences and work it out. Instead, they express dismay by granting one side a winning verdict while awarding the "winner" low damages. They send the message: "You both lose. No one deserves a victory."

In addition, a verdict that punishes deception does little to encourage honest relationships in the future; it punishes the wrongdoer for past behavior and ignores the possibility of a better future. In the case of criminal fraud, when one party is clearly anti-social, a verdict may be the best outcome that can be expected. In most conflicts, however, relationship factors should be considered.

But how does mediation handle deception? At first glance, it appears the less formal and less rigorous discovery is vulnerable to manipulation—the more amicable process opens the door to lies. It could be assumed the mediator's lack of power to enforce decisions further encourages deception. But these assumptions may be wrong.

◈

What role does a desire to expose deception play in this mediation?

Is the other party trying to expose your lies?

Are you trying to expose the other party's lies?

Should both parties consider identifying the lies of a third party?

DECEPTION & THE USE OF NARRATIVE ACCOUNTS

For the moment, set aside pathological lying and consider more common fabrications: *accounts* people use to reduce threats to identity and avoid sanctions. Accounts are the stories we tell to make ourselves feel better.

Typically, we establish a self-image aligned with our desire to be regarded in a positive manner; we seek to behave and perform in a manner consistent with our self-image. We try to maintain consistency between our self-image and our public image. When we fail to meet expectations, however, our public image is threatened, which undermines our self-image. When conflict arises as a result of our failure, our self-image is further threatened. In response, we skew our narrative account. We attempt to reduce the threat. As we all fail to satisfy expectations from time to time, we all experience threats to self-image. And thus the effort to present a positive account is common.

In our desire to render an acceptable account, we explain how we have fulfilled our obligations, performed duties, met expectations, and satisfied other tasks. But sometimes our misdeeds betray our desired positive self-image and public image: sometimes we fail to meet obligations or discharge our duties. Seeking to offset our failures, we create narratives that integrate failure and success. We attempt to Save Face.

Face-saving accounts are not blatant attempts to deceive, but rather attempts to manage self-image. We explain how we are not responsible for events that transpired or how we did not intend for our actions to cause harm. We insist the results of our actions are not as serious as they may appear; we diminish our culpability or reduce the assessment of damages caused. We explain away discrepancies between our positive identity and events.

Such accounts include: protestations of innocence; denial of involvement; denial of direct causality; excuses, justifications, and apologies; or a combination of the preceding. These are not objective truths but rather stories designed to protect identity. While, at times, we may seek to avoid sanctions by presenting accounts that minimize our transgressions, we should not overlook the role played by the equally important need to protect our self-image. We may be perfectly willing to suffer sanctions as long as our image is not seriously damaged. We accept our errors, as long as it does not impact negatively on our identity.

The accounts we offer are an attempt to weaken links between our behavior and prescriptions—laws, rules, traditions, commandments, duties, and responsibilities.[1] We explain how the rule or prescription did not apply to the particular setting, to the particular role we assumed, or to the particular circumstances in which we were involved. We take advantage of ambiguity regarding the prescription. We argue that while we knew there was a rule or obligation, we did not know it applied *to us* at *that time* in *that particular setting*.

Narrative accounts take advantage of weak or ambiguous prescriptions by citing a lack of clarity regarding prohibitions: "If the rule had been clear, I would have obeyed."

At other times, we claim we knew the results were unacceptable, but we were not in a position to control events and/or it was not our intention to have events turn out the way they did. This addresses intentionality, causality, blame, and sincerity.[2] People may argue that they were not a knowing and willing cause of harm: "It was out of my hands."

We construct an account that stresses the weakest link to the wrong we have done. The account the other party hears is colored by our focus on weak links. These accounts are not outright lies but rather a form of creative storytelling designed to maintain positive image. A frontal attack on the veracity of such narratives results in stiffened resistance to collaboration, increased defensiveness, and impasse.

For this reason, you will want to consider the other party's narrative account to be a rough draft. You should feel no need to judge its accuracy. The narrative is colored by aspirations and reflects how they would like to be seen; it is a conversation starter, not a closing statement. Consider the account an invitation to investigate how the other party constructs his world and protects his self-image. What appeared to be a fabrication may be a rich emotional response to adverse circumstances.

When an account is explored in a non-threatening manner, the originating party may feel safe to admit, "I didn't want you to think poorly of me. That's why I could not admit my role. I felt bad and didn't want to lose your friendship."

The party who previously thought the opposing party's lies were intentionally malicious may respond, "You care what I think? I had no idea you cared." The party dodging blame created an impression that was the opposite of what he felt — his narrative seemed evasive and telegraphed a lack of caring when that was not the case.

Rather than render a conclusion based on incomplete information, work with accounts like you would a Rubik's Cube, searching for a combination that brings clarity.

Fortunately, research confirms that apology is the favored account for easing past a dilemma.[3] When we apologize, we move from concern for Self Face to concern for Other Face. We tend to combine apologies with excuses and justifications used to weaken other links; this allows us to accept partial responsibility while lessening overall responsibility. We admit mistakes and accept consequences if we can maintain our positive self-image.

When you recognize the other's need to Save Face, it becomes easier to view a partial apology as a step toward reconciliation. You see deception as a defensive move to fend off emotional threat. When you treat accounts as a prelude to dialogue, you encourage flexibility and allow parties to discover that it is safe to be candid and honest.

You can manage deception best by turning to the future. When you allow the other party to deliver an apology in a Face-Saving context, you lessen the need for deception. A more candid narrative follows. When you feel that amends or reparations are warranted, you will have difficulty negotiating with the other party until you move past this face-saving stage.

⁓

In this mediation, will it be more important to assess blame for the past or to create a better future?

In what way does your account of what took place safeguard your self-image?

Is safeguarding their image important for the other party?

In what ways do you tend to justify your actions, particularly when you have been wrong?

Has your prior account of events caused an impression you did not intend?

Will it be necessary to revise your account of the events?

MORE ON HANDLING DECEPTION

When a party refuses to let go of deception, the mediator gently queries inconsistent narratives, contrary facts, omitted data, altered importance, dropped out time, and other artifacts pointing to deception. He does not level accusations, but queries whether the other party (or a jury) will understand the story being told. He points out inconsistencies and solicits explanations he can present to the other party to provide clarity. Or he asks the party how they imagine a jury will respond.

Mediation thus encourages rather than discourages change; we seek clarification, revisions and updates. We encourage a gradual move from deception toward honesty. Parties are encouraged to turn away from blame and shame and to embrace change and flexibility so the process can satisfy mutual expectations.

❧

Will you need to allow the other party to revise their account?

Will you rewrite your narrative to be more acceptable to the other party?

What about this conflict most threatens your Face?

What Face Threat might the other party experience?

What role will Saving Face play?

DECEPTION BY NEGATIVE THIRD PARTY

Our ability to lessen deception in the give-and-take of shared narrative accounts has one critical exception: when deceptive or false facts are inserted into the conflict by a hidden destructive third party.[4] When a destructive covert agent talks to one party and then to the other, spreading false information, the sly introduction of falsehoods creates impasse, as both parties assume incorrectly that they are relying on factual data.

The astute mediator pays careful attention to falsehoods designed to create animus between parties. He is alert to the possibility that a common (albeit hidden) source of deception exists. The destructive third party's presence may first come to light in the discovery phase, though most often it comes to light as a result of an impasse. This dynamic will be addressed later in more detail (see Chapter Twenty-Two).

❦

Has someone provided you with false information regarding the other party?

Has someone provided the other party with false information regarding you?

Is a hidden influence fueling this conflict?

Does someone harbor destructive motives toward both parties in this conflict? Who?

TWELVE

The Hostile Party

YOUR ADVERSARY MAY be committed to continuing the fight, committed to your demise. You may be entangled in a conflict with someone who is hurt, angry, and eager to attack. This portends increased difficulty, as trying to convene with a hostile opponent *on your own* is nearly impossible.

CONVENING WITH A HOSTILE PARTY

In order to convene with an unwilling or hostile party, a mediator may need to address destructive emotions. Prior injustices or failures to gain respect may have left a party with a negative view of reconciliation. He *knows* peace and love do not work and he *knows* he is being asked to compromise — and this time he is unwilling to give up the fight. His frustration, accrued over a lifetime of unresolved conflicts, is unleashed.

A mediator humbly offers to facilitate. She conveys an attitude of "my help might benefit you." She does not come to "save" the party and does not become defensive in the face of hostility and skepticism. She avoids the demeanor of the "expert from afar" sent to straighten out the unwilling party. Instead, she communicates that she is a trained professional the party may call upon to facilitate the reconciliation process.

When parties have been betrayed previously, however, promises of reconciliation ring false. The mediator, recognizing this problem, is willing to have her sincerity, commitment, and neutrality challenged.

⚘

How can you help the mediator convince the other party to

take part in mediation? What advice would you give?

Have you done anything that would cause the other party to avoid mediation? If so, what should you share with the mediator?

Are you reluctant to convene mediation? If so, what concerns should you share?

How might you convey to the other party that you are serious about considering their needs?

What concession might you take to the other party?

EXPLORING ALTERNATIVES

The hostile party is skeptical. Resolution seems impossible. A mediator candidly confesses that he cannot guarantee an outcome: uncertainty and risk are present; the process does not always result in resolution and reconciliation. He explains that the process *has* worked for others and, while not all parties enjoy success, a sufficient number have found satisfaction. The positive odds make the modest risk worthwhile.

The mediator queries alternatives: What is the likelihood other options will work? If you fail to resolve the conflict, what will be the consequences? He honors the party's assessment of the situation and validates their ability to make a rational decision.

Mediators explain that nothing will occur without party agreement. At first, the party will not readily accept this promise: adversarial and judicial models are too strongly imprinted on our psyches. Nonetheless, self-determinism becomes the primary persuasive lever: if results do not satisfy party needs, they can walk away. This pitch is so unique that it may take considerable work to achieve "buy in." Yet the promise that they will *not* be coerced into a resolution often provides sufficient comfort. They express willingness to explore the process *if* they are not forced to accept a pre-determined outcome.

How might resolution benefit you?

If you are able to resolve this conflict, what interests of yours will be satisfied?

What risk is involved in taking part?

What are the possible benefits of mediation?

What will motivate the other party to take part?

What needs must be met if mediation is to be worthwhile?

THE HOSTILE PARTY TELLS THEIR STORY

A mediator must possess a sincere desire to hear a hostile party's unique story—for no other reason than to satisfy her curiosity. We find it difficult to resist telling our story to someone who is genuinely interested. The mediator may say, "Whether or not you enter into mediation, my curiosity has been piqued. I must know what happened to you." She is a passionate student of human nature who constantly enriches her knowledge of human affairs.

What should the mediator do in order to gain confidence and trust?

FACE CONCERNS REVISITED

It is not uncommon to find that both parties sincerely harbor a desire to end the conflict, but neither can take the first step. Barriers arise from a fear of Face Loss. A reticent party may have announced they would never, under any circumstance, enter into dealings with their adversary, vowing publicly they will make their opponent pay for their misdeeds.

Hostility has taken on a public face. Efforts to reconcile represent a capitulation: to recant is to suffer Face Loss. The mediator blazes a Face-Saving path that allows the party to tell a new story, to rewrite a narrative both believable and acceptable to those watching. When the mediator publicly recognizes the party's needs, he also Restores Face.

❧

What gestures will the other party recognize as a sign of peace?

Has betrayal played a role in the conflict?

What will reestablish trust?

Has someone been insulted?

Has someone been ridiculed?

EMOTIONAL BARRIERS REVISITED

As obstacles are overcome and mediation becomes likely, you may experience unsettling emotions. You may find it difficult to imagine being in the same room with the other; you may experience physical discomfort that makes a face-to-face meeting impossible.

Conflict arms a minefield of emotional triggers. With a hostile party, it is too late to avoid triggering destructive emotions: those emotions are already hot and in play. The focus turns to finding ways to manage emotions. Destructive emotions are managed by setting an agenda in which less-threatening issues are addressed first, and more threatening issues are addressed once trust has been partially restored.

Even if you have been upset, hostile, and reticent to mediate, the wall of negative emotion usually dissipates when you discuss your situation with an impartial third party who listens. The mediator becomes a safe conduit for your communications. His communication skills substitute, temporarily, for your impaired skills: he models sorting out miscommunications and provides hope that such techniques can unsnarl the situation.

❦

What emotional triggers must the mediator avoid?

What emotional triggers must be taken up?

Should an agenda be drawn up that schedules less difficult issues first and more difficult issues later?

Or must the most difficult issues be at the top of the agenda?

THIRTEEN

Revenge

EVEN WHEN A party agrees to participate in conflict resolution, they may express a desire to "get even" or "make them pay." Desire for revenge is not something we easily push aside or ignore; we need to address our craving to make others feel the pain we felt. At times we find it difficult to admit that we harbor dark thoughts of vengeance; at other times we bristle and find it hard to check our cry for revenge. In either case, we find it beneficial to inspect our emotions and thoughts in order to bring them under control.

DETECTING & ASSESSING THE DESIRE FOR REVENGE

Unchecked escalation is a reliable sign that a desire for revenge is inhibiting conflict resolution. When we trade harmful deeds in a tit-for-tat exchange, we create a cycle of reciprocal revenge.[1] If these cycles of revenge continue, conflict will escalate to the stage at which each party is willing to destroy the other, even if they will also be destroyed. This dynamic — I will sacrifice myself to destroy you — is present in small measure at all stages of conflict. The logic of revenge — you should suffer as I have suffered, so that you will know my pain — becomes acceptable.

Revenge expresses our hurt: the most powerful expression we can muster is causing the other to feel the pain they caused us. A party who seeks revenge assumes the burden of his own future suffering in order to deliver a blow that ensures the enemy understands "this is how it felt to be hurt."

How might you help the mediator convince the other party to mediate?

Would you like the other party to experience the hurts, wounds, pains, feelings or consequences you felt, so they *know* how you felt?

Do you think the other party wants you to experience their hurt?

Has revenge been a factor in this conflict?

What painful emotions have given rise to a desire for revenge?

MOTIVES DRIVING REVENGE

We Need to Make Them Understand Our Pain

Revenge is an effort to make sure offenders "get it" and learn to care. We want the people who have hurt us to understand what they have done—in a visceral manner. We seek to "educate" offenders by causing them to suffer the pain they caused others. We attribute great importance to delivering the lesson: "this is how you hurt me." The desire is so strong that we are willing to sacrifice our safety and tranquility for satisfaction.

Our (mostly unconscious) calculation is that when the offending party experiences pain commensurate with the pain they caused, they will learn firsthand what they have done and they will repent. They will be forced to care—as *they* now feel the hurt. Revenge might be viewed as an attempt at enforced empathy; revenge aims to make the offender understand fully and care deeply.

When the offending party appears not to heed our pain, when their attitude remains hostile, uncaring or insensitive, the desire for revenge intensifies. If the offending party cannot or will not empathize with our pain and suffering, we deliver stronger retribution. We feel forced to increase their pain and suffering to the level at which they finally get it.

Unfortunately, pain and suffering do not bring increased understanding or heightened reason; pain and suffering blot out reason, abort understanding, and preclude empathy. Our awareness is diminished, not expanded, by pain and suffering; when we hurt or suffer, our focus draws inward and we become less perceptive and less able to learn. Though revenge rarely educates and enlightens our enemies, we still experience the need to make the offender understand how we felt when we were hurt.

Will old wounds need to heal before you move forward with mediation?

Will you require professional help in addressing harm you have suffered?

What do you hope to teach the other party by an act of revenge?

What do you suspect the other party would like to teach you through an act of revenge?

In the past, have you been successful in educating others through punishment? Why not?

We Need to Protect Our Self-Image & Identity

Many hurts are experienced as threats to self-image and social identity. Pride, our identity watchdog, mandates that every transgression must be avenged. Our pride in "who we are" depends in part on our ability to defend our identity from insult and injury.

Extreme transgressions that seek to completely destroy our identity, such as murder and mutilation, provide strong justification for revenge. Such egregious transgressions may even cause us to take revenge on behalf of another who is harmed. Most threats, however, are far less dramatic. They do not seek to end our existence. Nonetheless, lesser attacks diminish us—and we die in small measure. Our survival as the person we want to be is threatened. Ridicule and humiliation make less of us and diminish our sense of self.

Attacks on identity, even inadvertent slights, often evoke fierce responses; they trigger unconscious fear that our survival is threatened. When we experience humiliation or threat, we rarely seek empathy—we seek to defend. We respond with increasingly forceful acts of retaliation that demonstrate we have the power needed to maintain our identity and survive.

Revenge sends the message that we will defend our self-respect, self-image, social identity, and our existence against those who humiliate or harm us. Acts of revenge arise from our subconscious impulse to survive. As you prepare, inspect your feelings—make sure an insult to your image or identity has not inadvertently been transformed into a life-and-death struggle that demands you deliver a blow.

⤲

In what way might revenge help you restore pride?

Will the other party seek revenge in order to repair their self-image?

If you are unable to take revenge on the other party how will this make you feel about yourself? How might that be remedied?

We Need to Balance the Scales

Another motive is a need to balance the scales. We place transgressions committed against us on one side of the scale; we place the adverse consequences we intend to levy against another on the opposite side of the scale.

To achieve balance, it is not enough for Fate to deliver punishment: we must deliver the blow that restores equilibrium. Balance is restored by an act of revenge that satisfies our craving to deliver punishment for misdeeds. When a hurtful deed that was committed against us goes unpunished, we experience discomfort. Things must be set right.

When villains (those who hurt us) remain unpunished, we feel we do not live in just world. We find abhorrent the idea that a villain can cause harm without suffering consequences. It literally makes us ill. We too often assume the only way to heal that illness is to restore balance with an act of revenge; thus, a motive for revenge is the need to balance the ledger between wrongs received and punishment delivered. This parity is sometimes called "justice."

Have you tried to balance the scales?

Will there be a need to balance the wrongs done?

Will you suffer emotionally if you are not able to balance the scales?

We Need to Destroy Evil

The hurt we suffer and the reciprocal acts of revenge we desire to take usually play out on a small stage. Revenge may seem unwarranted. Nonetheless, there are also horrific acts of violence that offend the conscience so profoundly that it strains credulity to think there will be no revenge. The revenge motive in such instances may be a need to *destroy evil.*

We feel the horrors inflicted by thugs, terrorists, and tribal warriors must be avenged with annihilating blows. Only when evil agents are annihilated can we rest, satisfied that revenge has worked its magic. If we are honest, we find our inner narrative includes this desire to strike a blow against evil.

⁂

Does this conflict involve evil intentions?

Is there a need to confront and defeat evil?

In your estimation, what must be done to combat evil?

Do you believe the other party considers your actions to be evil?

We Need to Deter Transgressions

Revenge may deter future aggression when it stuns the other into ceasing their violence; in such situations, we believe that if the other party knows their aggressive actions will be met with brutal revenge, they will cease being aggressors.

This stance is often expanded into a preemptive strike doctrine that justifies delivering the retaliatory strike *before* a first strike takes place — based on the assumption that a first strike by the other party is inevitable. In more common situations, we may send threatening messages promising retaliation when we feel someone contemplates causing us harm or opposing our wishes.

⁂

What aggression will you need to deter?

Does the other party feel they must deter your aggressive actions?

In this conflict, has anyone used the threat of revenge as a deterrent?

We Need to Express Rage

Revenge also erupts from out-of-control rage. Revenge may be the result of violent emotion that overwhelms us during the period author Laura Blumenfeld calls "the boiling of the blood."[2] Overwhelmed by uncontrolled rage, we retaliate, striking out with little thought.

We rarely understand rage in the moment it occurs; hasty destructive acts can only be understood in retrospect, when we look back and plumb the depths of primal forces. With more than a tinge of regret we may recall our knee-jerk response to injustice. We were not fully conscious and in control and thus our acts become difficult to explain. Though we do not like to confess that we acted without reason, we know it is true. We may conclude that only a profound change in our character can prevent future bouts of rage.

Most of us pride ourselves on our composure and reason. This makes it awkward for us to admit that our behavior surfaced from the depths of our psyche like a malevolent stranger. Typically, we solve the dilemma by transferring blame for our actions to the other party. We dodge responsibility. While there is truth to the idea that the provoking party bears responsibility for the retaliatory consequences he suffered, we are aware that all too often we simply "go off." In the aftermath of such rage, we are left searching for one of two paths: either we take responsibility for our destructive outburst or we seek to dodge responsibility.

✧

In this conflict has anyone experienced uncontrolled rage?

What will need to be done to prevent uncontrolled rage?

Do you have a plan to manage your anger?

Have you been successful in managing anger previously?

Is the other party subject to outbursts of rage?

What will need to be done to protect against such rage?

What mediation guidelines should be in place to control destructive emotions?

UNRESOLVED CONFLICT PROMOTES REVENGE

When conflict goes unresolved, it gnaws at our good nature and leaves us in a constant state of irritation, riding swells of anger. We may act out our anger overtly, but more often we respond with covert attempts to annoy, humiliate, frustrate, or sabotage.

Frequently we take no action; rather we obsessively entertain thoughts of revenge. Our imagination gives us little rest as we conjure images of the suffering or demise of our antagonist. The clash may have started out as a minor difference of opinion, a response to an inadvertent slight, or a response to annoying efforts to dominate, coerce, or ridicule. From these small seeds of disrespect conflict escalates to the point where it ruins our life, steals our happiness, and leaves us seething.

During this stage of assessment, we seek to identify our hostile impulses; we seek to bring them into the open in an attempt to avoid out-of-control rage. We do not unearth our urge for revenge in order to honor it as part of our conflict resolution plan; rather, we inspect such hostility so we might transform it. When we allow destructive impulses to lurk in the shadows, they live for another day. Left untended they may later cause us to strike out during a moment when our "blood is boiling."

❧

Has a failure of justice resulted in a desire for revenge?

In this conflict, what would justice look like?

What does justice look like to the other party?

Has failed justice left you frustrated and fantasizing revenge?

What consequences will arise from acts of revenge?

What is the cost to you when it comes to taking revenge?

BEYOND JUSTICE-AS-REVENGE

In order to find true happiness, we seek apology, forgiveness, and reconciliation. We acknowledge where we stand at the present moment — we may have to acknowledge that we are not a forgiving person. So we take time to unearth such unpleasant traits. But, you might ask, should we not avoid digging up pain or hatred or other distasteful emotions? After all, our purpose is to restore happiness and contentment, not prolong despair. Avoidance, however, rarely bears good fruit. It is better to shine light on the actual conditions.

Is it our nature to engage in endless cycles of revenge? Perhaps. Walking away without exacting revenge leaves us feeling hurt and empty. But exacting revenge leaves us suffering burdens of guilt, remorse, and ostracism. The solution lies in skillful conflict management that transcends the dichotomy of revenge versus injustice.

What will shine light into the darkness associated with a desire for revenge?

How will you prepare to listen to the other party express their desire to get even with you for what they believe you have done?

What will you need to do in order to release dark thoughts that stand in the way of your ability to move on?

Will it be necessary to find additional processes to help release the pent-up hurt and anger associated with this conflict?

FOURTEEN

Stakeholders

MEDIATION MUST INCLUDE all stakeholders. Some stakeholders will have a direct stake in the outcome; others may be affected tangentially. As a first step, assess who must approve a settlement agreement. You will want to avoid negotiating a resolution only to discover that the decision makers are missing. The absence of those with authority to approve the deal may be inadvertent, or it may be a negotiating tactic—a tactic that allows "the boss" to insist on altering terms *after* a deal is negotiated.

Adequate planning defeats the "missing authority" tactic. Mediators secure a commitment to have all decision makers present or readily available. If another party springs the tactic on you after the deal has been negotiated, simply take the negotiated deal off the table and withdraw all prior concessions. Signal your willingness to start over. The reneging party usually realizes that the tactic puts them at risk, as the renegotiation may result in a less favorable outcome. This realization may make them reticent to continue the ploy.

Insist at the outset that those with approval authority be present to approve the deal; otherwise, it will become difficult to take a punitive stance toward the tactic. Likewise, if you are negotiating on behalf of a business, a community, or a nation with many stakeholders, determine in advance that you have authority to approve a settlement. Know your stakeholders' concerns before negotiating. If your authority depends on group consensus, design and employ effective consensus-building procedures.

Who are the stakeholders in this conflict?

Who must be present at the negotiation?

How will you become informed regarding stakeholder interests?

Will you have the authority to approve an agreement? If not, who will?

How will you make sure the decision maker will be available in a timely fashion?

What will you need to do to make sure your negotiating counterpart has approval authority?

How will you manage conflict among stakeholders on your side of the table?

Will conflict among stakeholders on the other side of the table threaten the resolution you seek?

FIFTEEN

Mining for Interests

IF YOU FAIL to identify true interests or if you fail to recognize the other's actual interests, negotiations hit an impasse. Frustration escalates and conflict persists.

POSITIONS VERSUS INTERESTS

Most people focus on positions that state, "This is where I stand." Positions or stances become rigid; parties remain locked in positional bargaining with little hope for a successful resolution. Disputants cling to their positions, seeking an advantage. Like wrestlers, they dare not alter their stance, as the slightest imbalance will allow them to be toppled. They appear to be frozen in place as if they were statues. They *can't* let go!

There is a solution. Mediators redirect the negotiation to focus on deeply held interests. Imagine a horizontal line: above the line, we have positions; below the line, we have interests.[1] Positions reflect our stance — where we stand. Below the line, we find interests that motivate our positions. Interests explain *why* we assume a position. The mediator may ask, "What interests does this position reflect?" Or, "What needs are you trying to satisfy by holding this position?"

❦

Draw a horizontal line. List your positions above the line.

Now list your interests below the line.

What are you trying to be, do, or have?

What needs are you trying to meet?

What interests are you trying to satisfy?

What are you trying to accomplish?

What identity is associated with that position?

EXPLORING INTERESTS

Often a person is not aware of all the many interests that motivate their actions: most likely, they have not clarified the relative importance of their needs and interests. Often, their position does not reflect their true interests. They push ahead based on untested assumptions that draw them into conflict.

During your preparation, when you explore below the line, you seek to deepen your understanding of your motives. You may soon realize the position you hold will not satisfy your true interests. This motivates you to decouple your current positions from your interests so you can explore alternative methods of satisfying those interests.

Most positions offer only one possible route to satisfaction; they possess a win-lose, all-or-nothing quality. When you lock into a position, you narrow your focus, letting that position dictate *who you are* and *what you must do to have what you want.* When the other party insists you *can't* have X—you want X even more. If the other party insists you *must* have X—you will not accept X under any circumstance. You become stuck in the oppositional embrace of conflict.

At that point, you abandon flexibility. You fail to recognize that your interests may be satisfied in numerous ways. You refuse to relax your stance, fearing the other party will move you off your position, delivering defeat. During your assessment, if you pay close attention, you will begin to recognize how much your position is dictated by the position your opponent holds.

In summary, above an imaginary line we find positions, while below that line we uncover the interests and needs that motivate positions. Our interests or needs are essential; they must be satisfied if we are to restore happiness. Positions are secondary and arise from underlying needs and interests. Thus, we must change focus from positions to below-the-line interests. As we relax our stance, our perceptions and creativity improve dramatically. We become flexible in our thinking, feeling, and communication, and we may cross over to sit "on the same side of the table" with the other party to collaborate on shaping a solution.

✌

Have you been forced by the other party to defend a position?

How would the other party describe your position?

What are the interests that motivate your current positions?

INTEREST-BASED NEGOTIATION

Another term for this model is *integrative bargaining*: we try to integrate all interests and needs into a comprehensive solution. This is often contrasted with *distributive bargaining* in which we divide and distribute available resources. Distributive bargaining has been likened to dividing a fixed pie; integrative bargaining involves "expanding the pie."

Distributive (fixed pie) bargaining is appropriate in many conflicts, but going "below the line" in an effort to integrate interests usually produces greater satisfaction and more durable outcomes. In negotiating an integrative solution, we expand the pie, the range of benefits available to each party. We look for creative solutions that satisfy the interests of all parties; we search for ways to add value beyond the dimensions of the fixed pie.

In their book *Getting to Yes*, Fisher and Ury propose that parties turn from positional bargaining to "principled negotiation or negotiation on the merits." This approach follows four suggested principles: "1)

People: Separate the people from the problem. 2) Interests: Focus on interests, not positions. 3) Options: Generate a variety of possibilities before deciding what to do. 4) Criteria: Insist that the result be based on some objective standard."[2]

Fisher and Ury champion the art of problem solving in which parties collaborate in their search for a creative solution. Interests become the pieces in a puzzle that we solve during creative problem solving. As we move from positions to interests, we are transformed from wrestlers into dancers.

Another factor warrants concern. A lack of negotiating skills may have precipitated the original conflict or blocked the path to resolution. When we are worried about our negotiation skills, we put off working on the problem or we make clumsy demands. Most parties, when introduced to the concept of interest-based negotiation, improve their ability to negotiate.

❦

Brainstorm ways you might "expand the pie."

How will you discover the other party's interests?

Will it be possible to separate the people from the problem?

Do you feel comfortable going "below the line"?

CHOOSING A NEGOTIATION STYLE

The integrative, interest-based, or principled approach typically produces the most satisfaction. In contrast, fixed-pie solutions promote win-lose frames of mind that make peaceful resolution difficult. Nonetheless, there are times when simple division of assets satisfies party interests; in these instances, the exploration of underlying motives, which is more time intensive, may not be necessary. There are times when one does not expect to maintain a relationship — in such cases a quicker process may be preferred.

It is unwise to adopt rigid procedural tenets such as "always engage in integrative bargaining" or "always seek to expand the pie." It is far better to tailor the process to meet the specific and unique needs that drive the conflict.

Has this conflict turned into a win-lose situation?

How might you transform it into a win-win situation?

Will a fixed-pie solution be most advantageous?

Or will benefit arise from an effort to expand the pie through collaboration?

NARCISSISM: SELF-INTEREST GONE AWRY

Narcissism is an obsessive need for esteem and self-aggrandizement. The narcissist is wholly concerned with self to the exclusion of others; he is selfish on steroids. The narcissist is unable to consider the other person's needs; he may, however, manipulate the other's needs to serve his own purposes. Our cultural emphasis on self-esteem and our lack of attention to sacrifice, giving, and collaboration promotes narcissism as a cultural norm.

The narcissist wants to possess the power needed to prevail over others. He asserts his rights and protects his self-interest. Narcissists are often unable to enter into good-faith negotiation; instead, they pursue a victory in court, imagining they will be rewarded thanks to the zealous advocacy of their attorney. However, such designs do not guarantee a favorable outcome in front of a jury. When a jury perceives that a party is unreasonable and disrespectful, they punish that selfish party. The narcissist, unable to jettison his me-first attitude in front of a jury, often harvests an undesirable verdict. Though the jury may feel his claim has merit, they punish the narcissist by awarding minimal damages. Paradoxically, concentrating exclusively on self-interest leads to poor outcomes.

An interest-based approach to conflict resolution exposes a narcissist: he is the party incapable of considering mutual interests. A mediator coaches the narcissist, nudging him to consider new perspectives, bringing his attention to the adverse consequences of self-centered narcissism. The narcissist may come to see how the success he feels he deserves can be achieved through collaboration, even though success-through-collaboration at first seems counterintuitive. This breakthrough in understanding can help overcome impasse in the negotiation.

❦

Has the other party been unwilling to consider your interests and needs?

Will it be necessary to make the other party aware of your interests and needs?

How will you convince the other party that it is in their best self-interest to negotiate in good faith?

Will the other party's narcissism force you to seek other ways of resolving the conflict?

VISIONING INTERESTS

There are many ways to mine interests. You can consult the literature on how to create and manage success, how to set goals, and how to maintain power. Such works may prompt worthwhile introspection. Too often, however, we fail to consciously identify and prioritize our personal interests. We bounce from situation to situation, from crisis to crisis, putting out fires while failing to build on our actual dreams. In many instances, the short-term goal of handling a crisis or gaining power and success obscures our long-term goals.

Robert O'Donnell of the Woodstock Institute for Negotiation suggests an approach that is simple and workable. List thirty vital interests, then allocate 10,000 points among the items, arranging interests in a hierarchy of importance that reflects your priorities.

In the world of drama, before actors put a scene on its feet, they identify their character's motivation by completing the thought, "I want to ..." They state the intention that becomes the actor's subtext, which drives the scene. In a similar manner, you can state the intentions inspiring your life using the phrase "I want to ..."

This list of intentions or interests provides criteria against which you measure whether or not a negotiated outcome is acceptable; you seek only those solutions consistent with your long-term interests. Too often we fight the good fight for a result that, upon further reflection, has no real importance. This vision list will help you determine if the negotiated solution really satisfies your interests. The following is an abbreviated example.

My interest is to... (I want to...)

Publish a book on conflict resolution	1780
Manage a successful mediation practice	1550
Practice my faith	1500
Train mediators	1435
Interview peacemakers	800
Fund a non-profit peace foundation	375
Consult with the local school board	250
Travel to sacred sites	175
...	125
...	100

Table 1. Interest List

Complete a rough draft vision list of goals.

Does this conflict concern an important interest?

Are there other ways to satisfy the interest?

Is this conflict worth resolving?

SIXTEEN

Making Decisions

AS WE PREPARE to negotiate, we seek to become aware of how we will make decisions, how we will predict outcomes, and how we will respond to risk. You will not become a professional negotiator overnight; nonetheless, a few basic concepts will increase the satisfaction you achieve in most cases.

This preparation still applies even if your dispute involves an institutional player, such as an insurance company — a frequent participant in litigated cases that go to mediation.

Institutional players may sport aggressive bargaining styles. They may attempt to set negotiation boundaries and dictate terms rather than enter into negotiation. Nonetheless, even insurance adjustors are subject to the concerns raised in this guide. When we negotiate with an institution, we often make the mistake of forgetting the human element present.

MEDIATOR ASSISTANCE

Mediators assist parties as they analyze offers and demands. They bring different styles to this task: they may facilitate, without offering opinions; they may evaluate, assessing possible solutions; or they may direct the process toward an outcome they believe is possible. Others nurture transformation that unleashes the parties' creative abilities.

&

How will you and your representative (attorney) work with the mediator?

Do you prefer your representative to take the lead or will you take the lead in negotiations?

How will your representative interact with the other party?

SETTLEMENT CRITERIA

At this stage, you call on your moral imagination and logical faculties to evaluate settlement criteria. This reflective step may seem tedious, but in the long run it saves time and produces superior results. When you identify the common errors that inhibit decision-making, you improve your ability to negotiate and thus satisfy your interests. Therefore, it makes practical sense to identify and remove bias and flawed reasoning during your preparation for negotiation.

COMMON ERRORS

Error #1: Accepting the First Proposal

Common decision-making errors sabotage our ability to negotiate a resolution that satisfies our needs. One error is *accepting the first proposal that satisfies minimum requirements*. We may jump at a solution that fails to satisfy the majority of our criteria—a solution that does not produce the greatest benefit. We may fail to explore additional options that might bring greater satisfaction. Perhaps we want to move as quickly as possible, as we are uncomfortable facing the other party. Rather than take time to process all relevant information, we race to get past the conflict. Or we may lack sufficient preparation, making us susceptible to accepting the first proposal that meets a minimum criterion.

How will you guard against the impulse to jump to accept the first solution proposed?

How will you keep in mind your desire to maximize your satisfaction?

Error #2: Eliminating Options that Fail to Meet All Criteria

The opposite error is *eliminating all options that do not meet minimum criteria*. As a result, we may reject all proposals, as it is rare for any one proposal to satisfy *all* criteria. Instead, we should determine which proposal satisfies the greatest number of criteria. We should assign relative values to the criteria and then compare them. Weighing choices in this manner slows the process and forces us to evaluate possible solutions. We do not seek scientific objectivity but rather the best subjective evaluation we can muster.

List the criteria you will use to judge the suitability of a solution.

Design a system of assigning values to possible solutions.

How will you carefully evaluate possible settlements?

Error #3: Using Flawed Shortcuts

In spite of our intention to be thorough in our analysis, we commonly employ methods that simplify and thus speed up decision-making. The mental shortcuts we use are called *heuristics*. These heuristics help when time is limited; however, shortcuts may become ingrained in our thinking. Eventually, we may become unaware of the inadvertent bias they enter into our decisions.

For example, we often make judgments based on our memory of *recent and/or vivid events*. When we compare the current situation to our experience, we often match the new scenario with easy-to-recall recent or vivid events. But such experiences may not provide an accurate model of current events. We may fail to consider how likely it is that such recent or vivid events will repeat. They may be anomalies.

This type of miscalculation may occur even when we carefully match the current situation to a more extensive recall of past experience. Such memories may not be representative. The decision we must make may not have a precedent in our personal experience; often our experience provides an inadequate sample of possible outcomes.

To arrive at a good decision, we may have to expand our knowledge database. We may have to consult with others who have faced similar decisions. When we take the time to evaluate whether or not our experience provides the information we really need, we prevent errors caused by inadequate sampling of possible outcomes.

What errors do you most frequently make in your decisions?

How will you make sure you have adequate experience and/or knowledge to make good decisions?

What research will you need to conduct?

How will you monitor your decision to detect possible error?

Error #4: Using Incorrect Reference Points

Good decision-making requires that we anchor our decisions to *relevant reference points*. Typically, we select baseline criteria against which we can evaluate a proposal. However, if the baseline criteria are invalid, we will commit errors.

For example, suppose we choose baseline criteria for evaluating our marriage based on our parents' relationship. But if our parents maintained peace by living separate-but-parallel lives, the baseline will cause us to miss an opportunity for a dynamic relationship.

The opposite can occur: we can set the baseline too high. For example, we may read a newspaper account of a hundred-million-dollar jury award in a high-profile case. Based on that article we may make unreasonable demands that will never be met.

There are no magic formulas for finding valid baseline references. Even with careful consideration, we may adopt a baseline that introduces error. Slowing the negotiation process, however, allows time for us to eradicate most obvious errors. If we are aware that personal bias distorts baseline references, we will take the time to explore baselines that others have used in similar situations.

⤔

What references or baselines will you use to evaluate solutions or outcomes?

Are the chosen baseline criteria adequate for assessing solutions to the current situation?

Will it be necessary to research common outcomes for people in your circumstances?

Is the other party using a relevant baseline or are they being unrealistic?

Error #5: Miscalculation Due to Overconfidence

Overconfidence causes miscalculation. We assume we can predict future events, but then we discover that our confidence is misplaced — errors accumulate when we use the familiar to anticipate the unfamiliar. Litigants frequently assume they will fare well before a judge or jury and then are surprised when the outcome fails to meet their expectations. One researcher found that "individuals are systemically overconfident in estimating the position of a neutral third party and in estimating the likelihood that a third party will accept their position."[1]

In addition, as conflict escalates, parties cease communication, creating an information vacuum. The lack of information allows parties to dub in an imaginary view of reality, which promotes overconfidence.

Personal narratives soon become self-serving. Each party considers that they have acted in a constructive and blameless manner. The information vacuum invites bias into their analysis of the conflict.

❦

Have you ever suffered from overconfidence?

Have your expectations been dashed?

How will you go about making sure you are being realistic when it comes to the outcomes that are possible?

Do you feel the other party lacks sufficient reality to make a good decision?

How will you promote the use of "reality checks"?

Error #6: Allowing Social Pressure to Increase Bias

Social pressure increases bias. Groups exert powerful influence over our thoughts and actions. A group may consist of legitimate stakeholders. If so, we should consider their needs. The opposite is true if we are faced with a group that does not consist of legitimate stakeholders. Their illegitimate demands may bias our decisions. If we act out of a need to appease a group that does not represent valid stakeholders, we may fail to satisfy our own personal interests. On the other hand, if we ignore legitimate stakeholder needs, our negotiation will be flawed.

❦

In this conflict, are stakeholders or observers applying pressure?

Is someone second-guessing you?

What group expectations might you disappoint?

Will you need to manage the expectations of friends and family?

Is the other party unduly influenced by social pressure?

Will you need to help the other party Save Face with his supporters?

Error #7: Becoming Overly Committed to an Earlier Position

Strident overcommitment to an earlier position is a common source of negotiation error. When conflict escalates, a party may overcommit to an earlier position that is no longer valid in light of changing circumstances. In the past, they may have taken a stand and vowed not to budge. Over time, they may have executed minor shifts. but with each new shift they issued a firm commitment to maintain that stance. They overcommit to a series of rigid postures.

Social psychologists note a common pattern in the shift to over-committed postures: "[A] party's concern with maximizing winnings, which was first replaced by a concern with minimizing losses, is now supplanted by a determination to make certain that the Other loses at least as much as the Party."[2] That position — *the other party must lose as much or more than I have lost* — becomes highly resistant to change. Overcommitment of this nature leads parties along the path to mutual destruction.

Review the wisdom of your earlier commitments. Determine if you have committed to a stance that no longer has merit. Make sure you are not anchoring your decisions to a baseline that is no longer relevant.

⚬⚬⚬

Do you feel locked into a position? Does change seem difficult?

What commitments have you made concerning this conflict?

Do you feel you cannot risk losing your honor by changing your mind?

What changes might you accept?

What changes in your understanding of the conflict warrant a change in your position?

Is the other party locked into a position as a result of a previous commitment?

Will the other party Lose Face if they reach a settlement with you?

How can you help the other party to Save Face?

Error #8: Engaging in Selective Information Processing

We commit errors as a result of *selective information processing*. We seek information that confirms our assumptions while ignoring information that counters our assumptions. Our bias—*I am right*—blinds us to the actual evidence. Unless we tame the propensity to view the world through faulty hypotheses, we will fail to maximize our satisfaction.

A playful way to understand this difficulty is to select a topic dear to you and then consider the ways in which you might be wrong about that topic. Most people can take only a few minutes of such torture. They would rather simply insist that their views on the topic must be accurate. They feel no need to dig too deep. Most people cling quite tenaciously to their view of reality without carefully re-examining their premises from time to time. This works fine until they become embroiled in a conflict, which forces them to engage in introspection.

One way to escape the *hardened reality dilemma* is to engage a trusted adviser as a critic. Choose a lawyer, counselor, friend, or spouse and grant them permission to challenge your views, assumptions, and biases. Grant them permission *to make you wrong*. Encourage them to challenge you. Their purpose is not to win the argument but simply to provide you with an opportunity to hear yourself argue. Though such role-playing is valuable, it is difficult. Allowing another person free rein to challenge your assumptions can be painful. You may not easily tolerate the emotional discomfort; however, if you can, you will benefit.

The one critic who will challenge your assumptions most strongly is the other party: they will use little tact in pointing out how wrong or misinformed you have been. Nonetheless, if you have engaged in the humbling process of having an adviser critique your assumptions, you will be able to assume a reasoned and humble posture. Your delivery will convey quiet confidence and certainty.

As a bonus, evaluating criteria and eliminating bias prepares you to identify the other party's decision-making errors. It allows you to better collaborate in evaluating mutually acceptable solutions. Your preparation makes you a better collaborator.

⚜

Do you assume the other party will not budge unless you admit they were right?

In this conflict has someone made you feel wrong?

Have you been insulted?

What will you and the other party need to do to set aside "I am right, you are wrong" thinking?

Is it possible that both you and the other party have been right about aspects of this conflict?

Is it possible that both you and the other party have been wrong about aspects of this conflict?

FACING RISK

Research shows people tend to be risk averse.[3] People tend to avoid risk. If they are given the opportunity to risk losing a *small certain gain* for the chance to achieve *a larger gain*, they usually decline. They walk away, satisfied with the smaller gain. If they are assured of a $1000 gain, they tend not to risk that $1000 on the chance that they might receive $3000.

People also tend to be *loss averse*. They abhor loss. Faced with certain loss, they will risk suffering even greater loss to avoid the existing loss. If they have lost $1000 they will risk another $2000 in an attempt to erase the original $1000 loss.

In summary, rather than risk what we have gained in an attempt to secure a larger gain, *we will protect what we have*. But, if we have experienced a loss, *we will risk greater loss* in an attempt to erase the existing deficit. We avoid *both risk and loss*.

In negotiation you may frame demands or offers as gains or losses. For example, imagine you are accused of damaging a property in an amount that has been appraised at $30,000. The other party demands $30,000, but you offer $20,000. How might the other party view this offer? As a gain or a loss?

The other party may view the $20,000 you offer as a $10,000 loss, as total damages were $30,000. They will refuse the offer and seek to secure the entire $30,000 — to avoid suffering a loss. To avoid a certain loss of $10,000 they will risk losing the $20,000 on the table. They turn down your offer and risk going to trial to obtain $30,000.

On the other hand, if they view your $20,000 offer as a gain they must protect, they will not risk walking away. The $20,000 is money they did not have before negotiation started. It represents a certain gain of $20,000. They will not risk that gain by going to trial. They will keep the gain they achieved.

Thus, a party can frame their offer as a loss or a gain. This affects the behavior of the other party. Mediators might advance both frames simultaneously, allowing a party to choose their own frame.

When you evaluate your offer from your point of view, the frame is reversed. You, too, can see your offer as a gain or a loss. Your framing determines how you will proceed. If you frame your $20,000 offer as a gain — because you are paying less than the full appraisal of $30,000 — you will not risk this gain by pursuing an even larger gain. You will not risk your gain by hoping a jury will make you pay less. Rather, you will lock in your gain and avoid a trial.

However, if you consider your $20,000 offer a loss, you may proceed to trial in an attempt to erase the $20,000 deficit. In order to avoid the loss, you are willing to risk even greater loss, as the court might award damages of $30,000 plus legal and other expenses.

In both cases, you offer the same amount. The only difference is the frame you attach to the outcome — do you see it as a gain or a loss? Framing affects your plans. Thus, when you prepare a rationale for your offer or demand, consider the framing. A poorly constructed rationale may cause the other party to refuse a reasonable offer. Or it may cause you to work against your own best interests.

Try not to force the other party to assume a negative frame. One article suggests, "Strategically, then, a negotiator should avoid inducing the opponent to make statements or behave in any way that would create the illusion of having invested too much to quit."[4]

How you will convince the other party that they have realized a gain they will want to protect?

What role will framing play in the negotiation?

How comfortable are you with risk?

What are your concerns regarding loss?

VALUES, BELIEFS, WORLDVIEWS

Values and beliefs are typically considered non-negotiable; nonetheless, be aware of the role they play in negotiation. When you start building bridges in earnest, you may discover that your worldview, your fundamental perspective on life, differs dramatically from your opponent's views. That difference may appear impossible to bridge. At first, you may assume the difference dooms mediation to failure; however, views that differ do not make resolution impossible. Rather, you must seek a shared resolution that is acceptable within opposing worldviews.

This is not easy, but not impossible. You will probably need to adopt *the core value of pluralism*, predicated on the Golden Rule: *Do unto others as you would have them do unto you.* If you want the other party to accept your values and beliefs *as valid for you*, then you must accept their values and beliefs *as valid for them.*

In contrast, when you assume that you must convince the other to see the world as you see it, conflict persists; when you force others to believe as you do, you seek to coerce their minds and hearts. You will want to make sure you do not have an unrecognized need to coerce or dominate others. You will need to ask: will such coercion really satisfy my interests, or will it inhibit achieving satisfaction?

On the other hand, if you practice reciprocity, you allow the other party to attribute their own unique value to solutions. You seek to agree on a settlement outcome, but not on the precise value you each attribute to that outcome; in other words, you and the other party may value the outcome for different reasons. In this way, you may arrive at a solution that works *in spite* of differences. This is not always easy, but you greatly increase the odds of a durable resolution if you acknowledge your opponents' needs *as they appear to them.*

Reciprocity dictates that you understand the other party holds values and beliefs that work for them, just as you hold values and beliefs that work for you. If change or transformation is required to bring about a resolution, the principle of self-determinism applies: if a party adopts a new value, belief, or worldview, they do so on their own determinism. You cannot force change. Rather you must allow change to arise from the other party's understanding of reality.

Pluralism honors diversity; paradoxically, it also provides the best opportunity for unity. When you abstain from coercing the other, you signal a willingness to collaborate. Respect for diversity draws parties closer; counter-intuitively, parties draw closer when they honor differences. Respect opens doors to reconciliation. Pluralism, reciprocity, and collaboration can be combined into a formula for negotiating in the presence of differing worldviews.

Nonetheless, there are times, such as when closely held values are challenged, that the inclusivity of pluralism may be hard to practice. When the ground beneath us becomes unsteady, when our core beliefs are under siege, we plant our feet firmly and hold steadfast to our position. When our worldview is challenged, we may experience alarm. We may resort to a righteous position that telegraphs: *take it or leave it*. This ultimatum is a symptom of a breakdown in reciprocity.

When reciprocity goes missing, you may refuse to engage in settlement efforts — as you know your values will not be acknowledged. The critical question you must answer is whether or not a principled stance will result in the best possible outcome. There are times when it may be wise to adhere to principle and forego a negotiated resolution — as long as you are willing to accept possible adverse consequences. If you are willing to suffer consequences (and are willing for others to suffer consequences), then the principled stand is valid. Too often, however, we fail to anticipate the consequences we must embrace.

In many cases, a decision to stand and fight usually results from a failure to fully inspect interests. You may not have asked: What interests are satisfied by the values and beliefs that make up my worldview? When you shift from a rigid perspective to a flexible and creative view, you overcome impasse. This does not mean you capitulate to the other party's demands; rather it means you negotiate creative outcomes consistent with your values.

✄

Is it easy for you to accept that others see reality differently? Are you comfortable with differing worldviews?

Will it be possible to reach an agreement even though the other party adheres to different values and beliefs?

In what way does the other party's reality differ from yours?

Is this a dispute over who will determine acceptable values and beliefs?

Are you trying to coerce another into accepting your worldview? Do you expect they will demand you change your view?

What role will reciprocity play in the negotiation?

BEST ALTERNATIVE TO A NEGOTIATED AGREEMENT

A "best alternative to a negotiated agreement" (BATNA) represents an "if-everything-else-fails" option.[5] The BATNA is the alternative if negotiation fails to satisfy your needs. A BATNA prevents you from agreeing to a bad deal when you hit an impasse and believe you have no option. The other party may seek to make you feel that you are out of choices, that your only option is accepting their offer. The BATNA represents the freedom to step away from coercion or domination.

A BATNA is worked out prior to negotiation. During the heat of negotiation, when tempers and emotions flare, when you worry that your needs will not be met, when you lose sight of the big picture — that is not the time to formulate a BATNA.

If you do not arrive at mediation with a BATNA, an overbearing opponent might argue that you have no other option: you must accept their demands. Feeling cornered, without a BATNA, you feel pressured to comply. Or perhaps, out of frustration, you walk away without a settlement. Entering a negotiation without a BATNA is a recipe for disaster.

A BATNA, the option you will exercise if negotiation fails, serves as an anchor in a storm. It is not a plan hatched in the moment but rather a well-reasoned, worst-case scenario with which you can live. It is also not a negotiating position, but rather what you do when negotiations break down; a BATNA does not function as a take-it-or-leave-it position that inhibits creative negotiation. Rather, it is the plan you put into effect *after* a negotiation fails and settlement is no longer possible. It is the plan you activate in lieu of a negotiated agreement.

When you have a realistic alternative, you do not lose hope and work against your self-interest. Instead, you are confident. You eschew making threats. The confidence that comes from having a BATNA will cause the other party to sense that you have a plan. They will feel your calm confidence.

⤲

Develop a best alternative to a negotiated agreement.

Is your BATNA realistic?

Can you execute your BATNA if negotiations fail?

BRAINSTORMING

Brainstorming is a technique used to expand options: you consider all solutions that come to mind, without evaluating their merit. You do not censor your thoughts no matter how outrageous or impractical. You may generate dozens of options with little value while seeking a genuinely unique solution. Brainstorming frees up creativity.

After brainstorming a pool of options, you engage your critical faculties and evaluate the merits of the options, selecting solutions that meet minimum criteria. In this evaluation step, you select two or three solutions that show the greatest promise, and then you re-evaluate those solutions in the light of new information you gain from the other party.

⤲

Brainstorm solutions with your attorney.

What might possible solutions look like?

Are you dealing with a multiple-part solution?

What barriers to creativity must be overcome?

FRAMING REVISITED

Parties often reject offers simply because they originate from the opposing party. In their mind, any suggestion offered by their opponent must be flawed. You can avoid this rejection by having the mediator frame a proposal as his own: "Here's an idea I would like to explore." Or, "I've been listening to both parties and I wonder if this idea might meet your needs." After the mediator reframes the offer as partially his own, the process moves forward.

Mediation motivates movement and flexibility. In a non-threatening setting, you are free to "test drive" solutions. After you release the oppositional embrace, you learn to dance rather than wrestle.

⨍

Will you need to have the mediator present your ideas for a solution to the conflict?

In what ways might a mediator reframe your offer?

SEVENTEEN

Negotiation

NEGOTIATION SKILLS VARY: many people lack training, while others are sophisticated. For those wishing to become proficient, numerous books and academic texts devoted to the topic are available.[1] While negotiation cannot be covered in complete detail in this guide, the following discussion introduces key concepts.

In negotiation, parties seek to exchange items of value, tangible or intangible, on terms suitable to all parties. They negotiate value they will *give up* and value they will *receive*. Balancing value exchanged is at the heart of negotiation. The exchange may involve tangibles, such as money or property, or intangibles like respect, status, power, or promises of peace.

Negotiation may also address previous give-and-take efforts that have gone awry; it is common to convene mediation to repair previous negotiations. The failure of an exchange agreed upon in an earlier negotiation is often the cause of a conflict we seek to remedy with facilitated negotiation.

DISTRIBUTIVE BARGAINING

Distributive bargaining is often called *the dance*. One party makes a demand and the other responds with an offer that, in turn, generates a new demand or counter-offer. The bargaining continues, back and forth, until parties arrive at an agreement.

Most of us are unskilled in this formal negotiation dance; past upsets may inhibit our participation. But you should not shortcut or skip the

131

process. The dialogue that accompanies offers and demands is vital for securing your satisfaction.

When you present a demand or offer, you typically present a reason. When the other party rejects a demand or offer or makes a counter offer, they usually express their reasoning. As you dance, you refine your understanding of the value assigned to tangibles and intangibles.

This painstaking back-and-forth process of negotiation leaves you feeling that you have created a fair exchange. The process provides certainty that you have crafted the best deal possible: you did not offer more than absolutely necessary nor accept less than necessary.[2] If you participate fully, you are no longer subject to obsessive second-guessing or post-settlement regret.

Timing, knowing when to make offers, is another basic aspect of the discipline. For example, you may wonder if you should make the first offer. While some negotiators prefer to wait for the other party to make the first move, others realize that the first number on the table, if reasonable, anchors the negotiation. The first offer, they believe, draws counter-offers toward that number, thus anchoring the negotiation.

There are limits to this anchoring effect: the first offer must fall within a *reasonable zone*.[3] Offers or demands outside the reasonable zone will be considered an insult and will be disregarded. This may slow or derail the process; thus, you should spend time in advance estimating the reasonable zone. If you are confident in your knowledge of the zone, go ahead and make the first offer to anchor the negotiation. During subsequent negotiation, you can rely on back-and-forth dialogue to determine a fair outcome.

INTEGRATIVE BARGAINING

When we adopt an interest-based style, discussion goes beyond dividing the pie. We try to increase the total benefits available in an effort to satisfy both parties.

For example, an employee desires a raise, but management states that their total revenue is fixed. A conflict emerges. The employee's need for greater earnings clashes with management's need to restrain costs. In an integrative bargaining approach, the employee might reveal his plan for significantly increasing the customer base, thus boosting revenues. Management might agree to underwrite his marketing plan and pay a significant bonus for new customers. If the plan is successful, employee and employer both benefit; they "expand the pie."

Integrative bargaining increases the number of possible outcomes. Focus turns to collaboration. Parties remove barriers to expanding the pie, adding value along the way.

Previously, before engaging in collaborative bargaining, you may not have truly understood how the other party attributed value to the tangibles or intangibles being negotiated. When you and the other party share your bargaining rationales, you increase understanding and then improve the deal.

❦

What help will you need with negotiation?

Will you primarily "divide the existing pie" or will you "expand the pie"?

How might you bring additional value to the negotiation?

What will you need to do to encourage the other party to join you in brainstorming creative solutions?

What intangibles or tangibles are on the table?

How might they be expanded?

SATISFACTION AS THE MEASURE OF SUCCESS

A third-party observer cannot accurately judge the outcome of the process. An objective measure of success cannot be found; we must rely on subjective satisfaction, which can be represented by a triangle whose sides represent substantive, procedural, and psychological satisfaction.

Substantive satisfaction concerns your satisfaction with the exchange of valuables, tangible and intangible. Did the outcome meet your needs?

Procedural satisfaction concerns the process—was it fair and just? Procedural satisfaction exists when you judge the *manner* in which the outcome was achieved to be fair and equitable.

Psychological satisfaction results when you feel that you have been treated with respect and that your emotional needs have been honored. When empathy for feelings has been shown, psychological satisfaction will rank high.

When you know the goal is satisfaction in all three areas, it becomes easier to prepare, as you know the objectives that must be met. You begin to focus on the substance of the deal, the procedure used to reach a settlement, and on your psychological needs as well as the psychological needs of the other party.

✒

How will you measure procedural satisfaction?

How will you measure psychological satisfaction?

How will you measure substantive satisfaction?

What do you anticipate you will need to do to satisfy the procedural, psychological, and substantive needs of the other party?

TACTICS

When we consider negotiation, we often think of tactics used to achieve an advantage. Should we be skilled in the use of tactics? Must we defend against tactics? When are tactics deceptive and unfair and when are they a valid means of reaching the best deal possible?

Some negotiators endorse aggressive, self-serving tactics, including deceiving the other party regarding one's intentions, as long as such deception does not cross the line into material misrepresentations. In their view, there is little call for transparency; a lack of transparency is considered necessary. Judging which tactics are proper can be highly subjective. While complete transparency may be overly idealistic, the intention to deceive the other is rarely the best approach.

The legal concept of zealous advocacy contributes to the dilemma. "The *Model Rules* adopt the hardline position that when negotiators make assertions about their settlement authority or the legitimacy of demands they are making, they do not vouch for the truthfulness of their assertions, regardless of how sincere they may seem. If a gullible person on the other side of the table believes a negotiator's false statement about a bargaining position, the fault lies with the person who is ignorant of the rules, not with the one who intentionally misleads."[4]

While some believe this zealous approach maximizes rewards, caution is warranted. If we argue that the deceived party is to blame for being deceived, then we must argue that trust plays no role in negotiation. The minute we abandon trust as a fundamental principle, however, we undermine the foundation of good-faith negotiation. When trust crumbles, systems built on trust cease to work properly. Willingness to negotiate and exchange value plummets.

Another article helps shed light on the purpose of tactics: "The essence of much bargaining involves changing another's perceptions of where, in fact, one would settle. Several kinds of tactics can lead to impressions that are at variance with the truth about one's actual position: persuasive rationales, commitments, references to other no-agreement alternatives, calculated patterns of concessions, failures to correct misperceptions, and the like. These tactics are tempting for obvious reasons: one side may claim value by causing the other to misperceive the range of potentially acceptable agreements."[5]

In a competitive negotiation, the idea of causing the other party to misperceive value seems natural. As you move toward a collaborative approach you see less need to cause the other to misperceive your intentions. Both sides benefit by gaining an accurate understanding of the value placed on tangibles and intangibles. The collaborative approach leads to more enduring settlements, as they are based on accurate information and clear intentions.

At the negotiating table, you must decide whether you will engage in tactics that better your position. Will those tactics be deceptive? Our natural inclination is to start on the competitive end of the scale. However, the relationship that develops during collaboration may change your decision. Empathy and compassion increase. Mutual caring and respect increase. As a willingness to collaborate increases, deceptive tactics feel out of place.

However, an inability to accurately state the value you place on something does not mean, necessarily, that you are being deceptive. We often engage in bargaining as a method of *clarifying value*. At the outset, you may believe you have a firm value in mind, but it is at best tentative. The final value is determined during give-and-take bargaining; true value emerges out of interaction.

The more competitive the negotiation, the more sense it makes to use tactics; the more collaborative the negotiation, the less sense it makes to use potentially deceptive tactics. The downside with deceptive tactics is the long-term adverse consequences. If you negotiate without truly considering the satisfaction of the other party, you are engineering an outcome that may not endure. Later, when deceptive representations come to light, confidence and trust are diminished or destroyed. Future conflicts become harder to resolve.

⤜

Meet with your attorney to discuss negotiation strategy and tactics.

What role will transparency play?

Is there a downside to the tactics you might consider?

Will restoration of a long-term relationship be important?

Will you need to build trust?

If the other party engages in tactics that make you uncomfortable, how will you respond?

Have previous tactics contributed to an escalation of the conflict? How might you repair such past upsets?

GOOD FAITH

In your preparation, write down your personal ethical rules for negotiation. Fundamental ethical axioms may include statements regarding the importance of trust, the need to avoid deception, the role of values, the need for reciprocity and respect. Use this list to draft process guidelines.

A common standard is called *good faith* negotiation. Good faith is somewhat vague but commonly assumed to include honesty with regards to facts and the absence of behavior that could be considered *bad faith*.

You may want to codify acceptable good-faith behavior after reflecting on the following issues and discussing them with your attorney: discovery procedures; frank and candid dialogue; confidentiality; procedures for disclosing positions, interests and concerns; private session procedures; confidentiality of private sessions; housekeeping issues such as schedules, locations and contact information.

While it makes sense to set procedural agreements in advance, this step can be overdone, stalling the process. It is best to adopt the minimum procedural guidelines required to enable the process to begin.

❦

Prepare a statement of ethical guidelines that provide you with a road map to a good faith negotiation.

Review the guidelines with your attorney.

EIGHTEEN

Managing Power

POWER CAN BE defined best as *the ability to affect the decisions, actions, and behavior of others*. When we desire a particular outcome, we attempt to cause others to act, think, believe, or behave in accord with our wishes.

A measure of the power you possess is your success in *intending* and *determining* outcomes. When you possess total power, you determine outcomes in their entirety — the resulting conditions are exactly as you wish them to be. When you lack power, conditions and events are not under your control — others do not act, think, believe, or behave in the manner you desire.

Most conflicts involve power struggles, contests over who determines specific outcomes; we wrestle over who will dictate conditions, events, actions, and behavior. Our mutual ability *to affect others* (use power) and *be affected by others*, plays a key role in conflict. The cliché "no man is an island" becomes painfully clear; conflict brings us face to face with the power of others.

Power is not intrinsically negative, but rather neutral; it is the manner in which you exert your power, for good or bad, that determines its value.

✎

During this conflict, what types of power have been used?

In what aspects of this conflict do you affect the decisions, actions, and behavior of others?

In what aspects of this conflict do others affect your decisions, actions, and behavior?

COERCION & DOMINATION

When you react negatively to the idea of power, you are usually responding to your experience with *coercive* power — times when force was used to gain your compliance. If you reflect on past conflicts, you will also recall using coercion to impose your will on others.

Direct application of physical force is not needed to coerce another; instead, you might issue a threat. Threats are an indirect use of force; however, later you may need to use direct force to enforce the threat. For example, you may threaten another party with penalties if they do not comply with a contract. If they fail to comply, you ask a judge or a jury to award damages; if the awarded damages are not paid, the sheriff uses physical force to confiscate the non-compliant party's property.

When others use power coercively, you typically become defiant or resentful. You chafe at the idea that your free will is trumped by another's power to constrain or dictate your choices and actions. The desire for freedom from domination and coercion appears to be a universal emotion.

When we become entangled in conflict, we become acutely aware of a loss of freedom: it seems that if we could only escape the other party's efforts to dominate us, we might enjoy a peaceful existence. This feeling of being coerced drives skepticism toward mediation: parties anticipate that misuse of power will render the process unworkable. They fear that raw power will be used to defeat their interests. In their view, they possess insufficient power; however, this is rarely the case, as mediation lessens power imbalance through the use of process guidelines.

The mediator guides parties away from coercive use of power and toward principled negotiation. Parties retain their ability to use coercive options if they fail to reach an agreement; however, as the mediator explains, overtly coercive means must be put on hold. He secures a process agreement that temporarily suspends the coercive use of power while parties explore alternative paths to resolution.

During mediation, you may discover that, although you retain your option to use force, coercive power will not help you meet your needs. A previously unrecognized downside to coercion comes to view.

&

In this conflict, has power been abused? Describe.

Have you attempted to coerce the other party?

Has the other party attempted to coerce you?

Have threats been exchanged?

Has the use of power caused resentment?

NEGOTIATING USE OF POWER

Power plays a significant role in negotiation, even if more forceful or violent expressions have been temporarily set aside. To shortcut non-productive uses of power, the mediator reminds the more powerful party, during private sessions, that coercive power does not exist in a vacuum — there are always consequences. He convinces the more powerful party to reflect on how a more conciliatory approach might lead to a satisfactory resolution. In the same manner, the mediator helps the less powerful party understand the consequences that accrue should they refuse to respect the more powerful party's interests.

On the other hand, weaker parties often have an unrealistic sense of the other's power, which can prolong conflict. Their miscalculations prevent them from engaging in productive negotiation. Often, when the weak party jettisons their aggressive posture, they discover that the other party has no intention of overwhelming them. Rather, the more powerful party has simply mirrored the weak party's aggressive demeanor. When a weaker party asserts power they do not possess, the other party escalates their show of power. A mediator, recognizing this counter-productive dynamic, orchestrates a face-saving dance that helps parties abandon a show of force in favor of more promising approaches.

As parties resolve their conflict, they often must negotiate future use of power. Their agreement may include provisions regarding future principled use of power to ensure compliance. If power has been abused in the past, setting agreements regarding future uses of power are critical.

In this conflict, does a power imbalance exist?

Has disrespect played a role?

How might the lack of respect be repaired?

Will the mediator need to address power imbalances?

Has power been used in a coercive manner?

Has resentment built as a result of abuse of power?

TYPES OF POWER

During assessment, we become aware of the *types of power used to affect decisions, actions, beliefs, and behavior.* The following discussion includes categories Robert O' Donnell of the Woodstock Institute for Negotiation identified in his paper, "A Different Look at Power."[1]

Procedural Power

Procedural Power arises from the use of organized procedures, guidelines, and processes. *How we proceed* affects our ability to control the decisions, actions, and behavior of others.

Procedural power is key in mediation: procedures and guidelines increase our ability to affect the other party's decisions, actions, and behavior. For example, when we tell our story without interruption, we are empowered to express what happened in its entirety, in our own words, with our own emphasis. The other party has the same opportunity. Reciprocal disclosure and listening helps us affect the decisions, actions, beliefs, and behavior of the other. Without this step, we are handicapped—if we have not been able to clearly express what happened and listen to the other side's version, we find it difficult to affect their views. After all, it is hard to affect someone who has not even listened to us!

Mediation *confidentiality provisions* empower us to better express our concerns. Frank disclosure, candid confessions, apologies, and expressions of regret that are made possible by confidentiality rules increase our ability to affect others' decisions, actions, beliefs, and behavior. If we cannot be candid with others, our ability to affect them is limited.

Well-designed procedures also increase our ability to alleviate fear of unexpected events. Instead, a well-designed process helps us anticipate the steps that will unfold. When we replace fear with hope and safety, our confidence is boosted, which improves our ability to affect others.

⸎

What procedures or guidelines will be needed?

What procedures have you found helpful in the past?

What guidelines will make you feel safe?

What role will confidentiality play?

Personal Power

Personal Power emerges from charisma, charm, honesty, integrity, likeability, humor, and empathy. Personal power draws upon virtue, conscience, and character.

Your deepest reservoir of power lies in personal power; and yet too often we fail to recognize the power within. When we come face-to-face with the other party, we may feel powerless; we may succumb to a low estimate of self-worth. Previous failed attempts to persuade others may have left us fearing that we lack required rhetorical tools. In the past, we may have extended a conciliatory hand only to have it rejected; now we may fear that our goodwill is insufficient. Nonetheless, if we have a cogent plan to increase our exercise of personal power, we can overcome insecurity.

There is good news. Your subsequent development of personal power does not depend on others. You can take charge of remedying the deficits that undermine your personal power. With hard work and discipline, you can bolster your confidence. You can nurture personality, charm, and humor. But personal power is not limited to social artistry. Additional qualities you can nurture — humble respect, calming empathy, and sincerity — play a strong role.

✐

What personal traits might affect the outcome?

How might you increase personal power?

In what way might the personal power of the other party affect you?

Referent Power

Referent Power derives its strength from reference to an external standard or source of power. A party may reference cultural standards of behavior, public policy, public opinion, or the laws of a state, nation, or international community. They may reference social or cultural benchmarks that dictate acceptable decisions, actions, and behavior.

Referent power relies on parties agreeing that external objective benchmarks apply. For example, the law provides formal standards that dictate what is legal and illegal, right and wrong. Less formal benchmarks dictate what is culturally acceptable or unacceptable. To the extent that legal or cultural benchmarks are considered valid or fair, they help to guide decisions, actions, and behavior.

If you disagree about the validity of laws, standards, or rules (or dispute their applicability to the instant case), referent power diminishes. It is not always necessary, however, that a party agrees with the benchmarks. For example, a court may enforce a verdict in spite of a party's protest. On the other hand, in mediation, if you or the other party do not respect a law, a rule, a standard, or an ethical precept, it is unlikely that referent power will factor into the *mediated* resolution.

During mediation, it is common for parties to reference the law and predict a jury verdict or judicial ruling. However, if opposing attorneys predict different outcomes, referent power is diminished. The party invoking referent power must anticipate how the opposing party will view the source of referred power; power is contingent on both agreeing that the referred source is valid.

Referent power may rise and fall. One party may be surprised when their opponent enjoys an unexpected surge in referent power, perhaps in the form of public opinion made known through protests or other public displays. An adversary who previously appeared powerless may suddenly command respect as a result of powerful support in the community. Power shifts of this nature require skillful handling.

Referent power has a dark side: peer-group pressure may enforce anti-social behavior. Gang members, for example, face internal sanctions for failure to persecute outsiders.

When negative referent power appears, a mediator seeks to promote inner change using a guided examination of consequences. A party is encouraged to consider how their actions solve a problem or make it worse. They analyze their values in the light of practical outcomes and within the context of creative problem solving. If they discover that their views are self-defeating, they may discard those views. The mediator helps them strip away false assumptions that are locking uninspected destructive beliefs in place. The mediator facilitates personal changes that help a party align their decisions and actions with positive goals.

✧

What standards or legal and moral codes will you reference?

Will the other party consider your referred standards valid?

What types of referent power will you use?

Will the other party challenge the validity of the standards you put forth?

What sources of standards or codes will the other party consider valid?

Expert Power

Expert Power uses information, skills, and knowledge to influence decisions, actions, or behavior. The expertise may be your own or may be solicited from outside sources, such as expert witness testimony or reports.

Expert power depends on party agreement regarding the validity of the expertise. How credible is the expert? Imagine driving a car toward a precipice with a world-class expert in the backseat providing information on braking distance. You are likely to plummet off the cliff if you make a mistake, so you listen closely to the expert and apply the brakes in a timely fashion. His expertise — his ability to predict consequences — affects your decisions, actions, and behavior.

The other party may accept an outside expert witness. However, it is more difficult to convince the other party that your personal expertise is valid. Nonetheless, do not give up. There are times when your expertise will carry weight. You might argue, "I've been there. I've done that. And I can assure you from personal experience that if you do X the result will be Y." The confidence and sincerity you display may be persuasive.

In another version of expert power, your valuable knowledge or skills might be exchanged as part of a negotiated settlement. For example, you may convince a high-level manager to grant you the autonomy you desire to run your department without interference. The current dispute over your autonomy resolves when your expertise is acknowledged.

Self-knowledge, though less obvious, should be considered. A person lacking self-knowledge waffles in the face of opposition. Lacking knowledge of his actual interests, he finds it difficult to make decisions: he appears weak and ineffective. He may sacrifice his interests when faced with a self-confident opponent. In contrast, if he had gained self-knowledge, he would be able to affect others with a calm self-confidence.

~

What matters might be settled using expert opinion?

Will it be necessary for you to demonstrate expertise?

How will you convince the other party that your expertise is valid?

What outside experts will you solicit to provide testimony?

Will you and the other party jointly access the services of an expert?

In what ways can you increase your self-knowledge in preparation for negotiation?

Resource Power

Resource Power concerns resources such as time and money — resources that influence the conflict and proposed settlements. Resource power arises from assets, tangible and intangible, that a party marshals for the purpose of resolving the conflict.

Resource power may play a positive role when it comes to underwriting a settlement. On more than one occasion I have seen a party who possessed ampled resources demonstrate patience and compassion. They would not have been able to show such patience if they had lacked resources.

In some instances, however, a party with fewer resources dictates the actions of a party with superior resources. The lack of resources leaves the resource-poor party unable to compensate the damaged party; they are unable to properly resolve the dispute by making good on obligations. In this scenario, the party with superior resources faces a loss and peaceful resolution depends on creative negotiation of alternative means of restitution.

In negotiation with large institutional parties, such as insurance companies, the institution clearly has overwhelming resource power, creating an imbalance. In such cases, you will want to engage other types of power in your attempt to balance the negotiation. Too often we forfeit our interests and fold up in the face of such power imbalances—when what we need is a creative way to bring other types of power to bear. Often, we overlook the manner in which personal power, coupled with ethical and referent power, can be brought to bear on the situation.

Allocation of resources is usually the focus of negotiation. Thus, you will want to complete a thorough assessment of the resources available, and you will want to anticipate how the other party will use resources.

❧

What resources will be necessary to see this dispute to the end?

What resources are you willing to commit?

Will the other party's resources be a factor, positive or negative, in this negotiation?

Will you need to offset the other party's superior resources with other types of power?

How might you increase the resources you can commit to this dispute?

Exchange Power

Exchange Power arises from an ability to trade or swap one valuable for another. The creative give-and-take of negotiation may be foreign to you, perhaps even threatening. In an effort to offset this deficit, you may enlist the services of a lawyer or you may undertake a study of negotiation. (Keep in mind that the mediator facilitates the negotiation and cannot ethically negotiate on behalf of one party.)

Exchange power depends on an orderly process in which parties can explore their respective needs. They must feel safe in the hope that a valid give-and-take is possible. They must feel that the exchange of one value for another will satisfy their interests.

In many cases, you might not recognize the value you possess that the other party needs. However, when you explore mutual needs, you may become aware of potential exchanges. During negotiation, it may help if you understand what it is that you possess that will affect the decisions, actions, and behavior of the other. What do they need?

Exchange power depends on trust in the medium of exchange; for example, we must trust that the currency used will retain its value. In societies that possess a stable currency, exchange power leads to prosperity. Exchanges of value can take place easily with a high degree of trust.

In contrast, when confidence in the medium of exchange wanes, exchange power dwindles. When the medium of exchange is compromised, the give-and-take grinds to a halt. Likewise, exchange power may be constrained by prior breaches of trust that need repair. In mediation, trust is repaired and confidence built; then an exchange is negotiated.

~

Are you comfortable with your negotiation skills?

Will you need additional training?

Will you need to be represented by a professional negotiator?

What tangibles or intangibles do you expect the other party will want to exchange with you?

Do you fear the other party will take advantage?

How will you go about assigning value to the tangibles or intangibles exchanged?

Have there been previous problems with exchange that will affect this negotiation?

Reward Power

Reward Power employs a reward, an extra value awarded for performance beyond normal. A reward is an inducement. It reflects an increased desire on the part of one party to bring about a decision, action, or behavior on the part of another.

The party offering the reward may not wish to pay the amount the other demands — unless their performance rises above expectations. So the exchange includes a performance reward. A reward may be valuable when negotiations stall. One party may agree to increase their offer but only as a reward for exemplary performance. They sweeten their offer on a conditional basis.

A reward may represent a contingent show of respect, in anticipation of that respect being earned. The reward may be offered as an inducement intended to overcome a history of non-performance. A reward may simply acknowledge that a party is about to perform beyond the ordinary — for example, delivering an order in a shorter time period than normal. A reward can be an acknowledgment of the challenges faced in meeting terms — it acknowledges that the demands are difficult to satisfy yet signals that the party offering the reward does not intend to take advantage of the situation.

Rewards deserve caution. The party to whom the reward is offered may consider the gesture disrespectful; they may consider a reward reflects a low estimate of their motivation. To avoid this problem, a reward should be framed in a positive manner, avoiding the impression that one doubts the other party.

❦

Will it be necessary to offer a reward to induce the other party to satisfy your interests?

How will you make sure you send the right message regarding rewards?

Will someone need to do something extraordinary to resolve this conflict?

Hierarchical Power

Hierarchical Power uses senior position or superior status to influence the decisions, actions and behavior of those holding subordinate positions or inferior status.

Hierarchal power, with its inherent imbalance, can be abused. Its use requires considerable skill, as the lower-status party may feel powerless, which leads to resentment, which often causes them to use covert means to exert their will.

A naïve executive may fail to discover that the sabotage ruining his best plans represents a covert reaction to his hierarchal power. He may fail to attribute a downturn in business or productivity to the covert response to his power. Tyrants who use hierarchal power indiscriminately end up having to use greater and greater force to protect their position. They (correctly) imagine that those over whom they exert power have become covert enemies, assassins looking for an opportunity to destroy them. They do not recognize that they have engineered their own demise with their abuse of power.

Hierarchal power is not always abusive or dangerous. There are legitimate, practical reasons to operate within hierarchal structures. An organization with a clear command structure is efficient. Confusion that results from diffuse and unclear leadership is avoided. However, trouble results when hierarchal power exceeds its utility, leaving subordinates feeling powerless.

We can diminish abuse by placing limits on hierarchal power; we conform position and status to the purpose of the organization. Boundaries that limit power arise organically from purpose. When leaders expand their power beyond that needed to realize group goals, they stray into abuse of power. Structuring hierarchal power around a known and recognized purpose generates respect for legitimate power.

Conflicts regarding hierarchal power require delicate handling. Parties must respect status and position, yet not abandon their needs. The party with lesser status avoids challenging Face; they must tactfully muster other types of power to remedy any imbalance. They must skillfully represent their own interests while respecting the Face needs of higher-status individuals.

Likewise, a party with superior hierarchal power must not use position or status to sabotage the conciliation process. When negotiation becomes challenging, as it usually does, they must not use their power to bail out prematurely. If the higher-status party fails to see the process to completion, the lower-status party departs harboring resentment that later manifests as covert non-compliance.

One way to address unequal status is to focus strictly on respective interests. The mediator facilitates discussion of how the lower-status individual can achieve satisfaction at the same time the higher-status party also satisfies interests, all within the context of organizational purposes and goals. Strict adherence to interest-based negotiation aligned with goals and purposes overcomes most liabilities associated with mixed-status negotiation.

On occasion, the focus may be on remedying abuse of hierarchal power: misuse of position or status may push an organization to the brink of ruin, necessitating intervention. New agreements or structures may be required to check abuse. Given that the previous structure resulted in abuse of power, parties explore restructuring the organization or group to discourage future abuse.

Problems also emerge when a higher-status person assumes those with less power naturally resent his status and will rebel regardless of his actions. While he assumes people are inherently rebellious, people with lesser power actually appreciate hierarchal structure, preferring a leader who guides the ship with a steady hand. Resentment most often is confined to abuse of power that robs people of self-respect, dignity, and opportunity. When abuse is present, the personal style of the higher-status person may become the central issue.

When position or status is challenged, conflict resolution focuses on the breakdown in consensus, on the cessation of willingness to grant allegiance to the leader. If lesser-status individuals no longer consider the position or status valid, they will fail to comply. They may challenge authority. Hierarchal power depends, at least in part, on a perception that the higher-status person deserves power: status must be earned. When this is not the case, the situation must be reappraised.

The subject of granting and maintaining status, position, and hierarchal power consumes many top organizational minds. There is a variety of opinion on how to best structure and operate a company (country, city, or household). Management experts engage in endless speculation regarding how to best govern collective efforts. This makes negotiation involving position and status lively and challenging.

❦

In this conflict, has power been abused?

Does this conflict involve a difference in position or status?

Has position or status been used in a coercive manner?

Has a lack of clear lines of authority created confusion and conflict?

How will power be used in a respectful manner?

How will you show respect during this negotiation?

How will abuse of power, if any exists, be remedied?

Is the use of power aligned with the purpose of the organization?

Punishment Power

Punishment Power may involve brute force, which is used to constrain, confine, imprison, injure, or destroy another party. It may involve a third-party, such as the police. Or punishment may be subtle, such as blocking fulfillment of the other party's desires or wishes.

Punishment power functions most often in conjunction with other powers: a boss turns hierarchal power into punishment power when he fires an employee; a party with resource power punishes another financially with a protracted and costly legal battle; a party with personal power uses public scorn and disrespect to cause embarrassment or exclusion; a party with referent power censors another and excludes them.

Punishment has a coercive nature. For this reason, a mediator facilitates understanding of possible adverse consequences, including a destructive backlash. O'Donnell notes that punishment power is very costly to the one who uses it, as it most often causes resentment and revenge.[2] Mediation may be rendered impossible in the wake of punishment, foreclosing on the possibility of a negotiated resolution.

One characteristic of punishment is desperation. The punisher typically has failed to control the decisions, actions, or behavior of the other. They resort to punishment out of desperation. A deficit of other types of power leads to the use of punishment; for example, lacking other types of power, a bully resorts to brute force to punish his victims.

Wars often begin with frustration over an inability to bring about change, compliance, or agreement; the frustration gives rise to a desire to punish an enemy. In his desperate acts of violence, the terrorist attests to his lack of power. The criminal justice system reflects societal desperation: the criminal, it appears, will not respond to other types of power, provoking punishment. Thus, to understand the use of punishment, we may analyze prior failed attempts to use other types of power.

Paradoxically, a party's refusal to *respond* to other types of power may arise out of their inability to *use* other types of power. It appears a party must be able to exert power over others before they respect that same power applied to them. The person may (unconsciously) assume that if they cannot use the law to curtail the unwanted behavior of others, they should not allow the law to curtail *their* actions. A party unable to use more subtle types of power may not respond when others use subtle power.

It is also common for a party to need help remedying past upsets regarding misuse of punishment power. Mediation may stall until the upset associated with previous punishment is fully handled.

⚮

Has punishment been used in this dispute? What happened?

Have you considered punishing another? What will happen if you do?

Has another considered punishing you? What will happen if they do?

Has desperation led to the use of punishment?

What alternatives exist?

Will you need to remedy past upsets regarding punishment?

NINETEEN

Use of Power

IN THE PREVIOUS chapter, power was defined as *the ability to affect the decisions, actions, and behavior of others*. Power could be measured by our success in intending and determining outcomes.

As our purpose in preparing for mediation is to satisfy our interests, it makes sense to spend additional time reflecting on how we will bring others to act, think, believe, or behave in accord with our wishes.

How we will use a type of power is often apparent in its description. When we use exchange power, we trade valuables; when we use referent power, we refer to outside standards or collective values; when we use punishment power, we punish the other party. There are times when the connection is not as clear. Consider the following suggestions and then add categories of your own.

COERCE

You can use force, direct or indirect, to coerce another to act or behave as you wish. With coercion you negate the other party's efforts, rob them of their self-determinism, dismiss their interests, discount their humanity, and make nothing of them. You can use force to compel the other to be who you want them to be, do what you want them to do, and have only what you want them to have.

Though you may overwhelm the opposition in the short run, in the long run coercive force inspires others to use coercive force and prompts revenge. If we extrapolate the consequences of using brute force, a picture of widespread destruction emerges. Entire civilizations crumble. Negative consequences accrue at the personal level: relationships and lives are destroyed. The cost of coercion, in the long run, is almost always prohibitive.

❦

Will you need to use coercive force?

How have you used force in this conflict?

Has the other party used force? Describe.

Will it be necessary to address harm caused by the use of force?

THREATEN

The use of a threat may appear to be a valid way to exert control, but significant potential liability exists. Once threats have been used, building bridges becomes more difficult. Threats escalate the conflict; eventually mutual destruction appears justified.

When you issue a threat, the other party may counter with a threat; a tit-for-tat response is a common. Furthermore, when you issue a threat, you harden your own position needlessly; you feel you must back up your threat to Save Face. Inadvertently, when you issue a threat you set up a situation in which you must carry out the threat or Lose Face.

A more effective approach is to discuss possible adverse consequences without issuing threats. Calmly and rationally describe consequences that will emerge. If the outcomes you describe in a calm and logical manner appear to the other party to be a threat, ask them how they would respond *if they were in your position*. Invite them to explore what an appropriate response to their behavior would look like. Connect the cause-and-effect relationship between their actions and your responses.

Threats present another liability: when a threat is issued, it becomes difficult to separate the threat from the person making the threat. The focus turns from interests to people—the exact opposite of what we hope to achieve in principle-based negotiation. After you issue a threat, the other party casts you in their story as a threatening enemy. They have a difficult time seeing you as a collaborator; they see you as a villain.

A threat is a notice of a future consequence delivered with anger. It invites the other party to resume their opposition. Its use warrants caution.

❦

In this conflict, have threats been used?

Will it be necessary to address the previous use of threats?

Will you Lose Face if you fail to deliver on a threat?

Does the other party fear losing Face if they do not make good on a threat?

How will you explain your willingness to mediate in light of previous threats?

How will threats be avoided during negotiation?

MANIPULATE

With manipulation, we try covertly to satisfy our interests at the expense of the other party. A master manipulator achieves his goals with little or no concern for others. Some people see virtue in manipulation; they even blame the party they manipulate for not being smart enough to catch their duplicity. In their view, if you are cheated, you *deserve* the loss because you failed to protect yourself.

This view posits manipulation as the natural state of affairs and advances the axiom: "to the skilled manipulator goes the spoils." In their view, manipulation has positive value: it maximizes self-interest. Satisfying the interests of the other party is not part of the calculation. As you enter negotiation, it pays to assess whether or not you are dealing with someone who believes they have a right to engage in manipulation.

Manipulation has drawbacks. Over time the manipulated party becomes angry over the hurt they have suffered. They refuse to remain in the relationship. As trust disappears, the friendship is abandoned. The manipulator has an increasingly difficult time convincing others to trust him. Those who have been manipulated conclude that it is best for them to do business only with people they know well. This increases the value and power of social networks, as they provide a firewall against manipulation.

After society has been the victim of widespread manipulation for a period of time, the general trust level plummets. People become defensive and cautious. It becomes much harder to engage in productive activity due to the increased need for vigilance. Multiple layers of security are required. The culture experiences an overall downward spiral in prosperity. When a culture values deception and trickery, when the deceiver and the manipulator become folk heroes, hard times lie ahead.

✌

Has manipulation been a factor in this dispute?

Have you been tricked or deceived?

Have you deceived the other party?

What agreements will prevent manipulation?

Will previous manipulation need to be addressed?

How might you use communication skills to prevent manipulation?

GIVE UP OR GIVE IN

Giving up or giving in may seem counterintuitive, but as O'Donnell notes, when you give in, you leave the other party feeling they owe something in return, something to be paid in the future.[1] Yes, there are times when giving in does not produce a beneficial effect: the other party takes advantage and you feel abused. At other times, however, the other party feels obligated and attempts to reciprocate.

Sometimes, after you give in, the other party may feel they have taken unfair advantage. They feel they must make amends. The time frame of this urge varies greatly. The response may be immediate; the other party may make a new offer that better satisfies your needs. This quick reversal arises out of a sudden recognition that they are about to cause harm — and they do not want the burden of committing an injustice.

In other cases, the realization may take years or even decades. You may have to wait until the party recalculates their moral balance sheet. You must be patient and seek equity in the long term.

Our natural tendency is to *want those things we cannot have and reject those things we must have*. This dynamic plays a role in "give up or give in." When you desire something, the other party is drawn to oppose your wish. As long as they are able to deny your satisfaction, they fight. But once you give up, they feel compelled to reverse direction. Once you announce you no longer want something, they reverse course and want to help you. This reversal is not a conscious response; rather, it is a natural but unconscious response. It is very mechanical.

These dynamics can be observed when children fight over a toy. When the disappointed child gives up and walks away, the child withholding the toy reverses behavior and tries to share. He or she may even force the previously hoarded toy on the other child. This dramatic reversal demonstrates the principles of "give up or give in."

❧

Where have you focused resistance to the other party?

What might happen if your resistance or holding on suddenly disappeared?

What response do you anticipate if you were to give in?

DEFER

Your use of power can include going to a third party for a decision or verdict the other party will be forced to accept. This parallels referent power, as it is an appeal to a higher authority such as the courts.

EMPOWER

You can entrust the decision to the other party. This approach differs slightly from giving up—as you remain engaged but transfer power over the outcome to the other party.

Holding your power in abeyance while trusting the other party may seem counterintuitive: how do you use power by *not* using power? One aspect of all conflict is the struggle over the right to dictate what will happen. This latent power struggle percolates below the surface. If you temporarily relax control over decision-making, the struggle subsides. In this approach, you put the decision in the hands of the other person, thereby abandoning the struggle for control.

The result can be surprisingly positive. When the other party feels respected and trusted, they often feel a need to reciprocate and satisfy your interests. When you relax your need for control, the chronic oppositional embrace is released.

This works especially well when the other party harbors suspicions that you are not really ready to collaborate. When you relinquish control, trust increases. Paradoxically, to achieve your desire, you let go of your desire.

❧

What aspects of the negotiated outcome might you entrust to the other party?

Are you clinging to control you no longer need to exert?

How might you turn the other cheek in a show of non-resistance?

Has there been a fight over who will exercise control?

INFLUENCE

The use of influence is a vital tool. One school of mediators specializes exclusively in the study of influence, as taught by Robert Cialdini.[2] Drawing upon research in social psychology, Cialdini explains influence factors such as reciprocation, commitment and consistency, social proofs, liking, authority, scarcity, and automaticity. If you feel awkward or unprepared to negotiate, his introduction to the use of influence is an excellent place to begin your study.

Influence calls on intangible relationship skills. Parties may come to the table with hierarchal, resource, or expert power but then squander those powers as a result of inept use of influence. They may be totally unaware of the influence they wield. On the other hand, those who grasp the subtle skills of influence tend to have greater success in satisfying their interests.

How will you influence the decisions of the other party?

How might the other party attempt to influence your decisions?

How might you become more successful in using influence to satisfy your interests?

PERSUADE

We can persuade the other party to accept our position with evidence, facts, logic, or other convincing presentations that support the merit of our position.

During facilitated negotiation, offers and demands are exchanged. They are accompanied by reasons *why* we should accept the offer or demand. An offer or demand proffered without a reason is easily swept aside and often triggers resentment. Attaching a reason to the offer communicates respect and acknowledges the other party's self-determinism.

Sometimes, however, reasons may not be the key factor; you may be swayed by emotions or intuition. Nonetheless, even when emotions or intuition drive your decision, a persuasive reason allows you to feel comfortable with your decision. Though your decision may be based entirely on emotion, you want to feel *as if* you acted rationally.

This is especially true when you must report to friends, family, a boss, or other stakeholders. It is easier to explain your actions on the basis of a logical reason, even if that reason was tangentially involved in your decision. Thus, it is wise to prepare to offer persuasive reasons — even if the real motivation is less logical or reasoned.

Your ability to affect the other party (your power) increases when you are clear regarding the logic of your decision-making. This works in reverse as well. If you worry that the other party is deceptive, you ask them to clarify the logical principles on which they are operating. You draw them into a dialogue that requires a clear statement of their intention. Subsequently, you can persuade them to remain consistent with their logic and principles.

❧

Have your previous attempts to persuade the other party failed? If so, why?

Has the other party tried to persuade you their view is correct?

How will you persuade the other party your views are correct?

How important will a rational reason be?

Will you need to provide the other party with reasons for accepting a deal?

COMPROMISE

Compromise, like collaboration, is a way to exercise power. For example, we may have resources that allow us to take a partial loss and bring the conflict to an end, so we can turn our attention to more productive endeavors.

You may reach a moment in negotiation when you realize your aspirations will not be fully met: your interests simply cannot be fully satisfied with the resources available. Or you discover that the goodwill of the other party has boundaries you did not anticipate. It becomes clear that full integration of your interests with their interests is not possible. Turning to compromise, both parties walk away partially satisfied and partially dissatisfied.

Compromise is most useful when you do not expect the relationship to continue; it works best when the end of the conflict is also the end of the relationship. You accept partial dissatisfaction in exchange for the psychological satisfaction of release from the burden of conflict. In relationships that are expected to continue, however, the desire to avoid lingering dissatisfaction may warrant spending the extra effort needed to find a collaborative outcome.

❦

Does compromise provide an advantage in this dispute?

Have you tried to compromise in this dispute? What happened?

How might a compromise be structured?

Is it more important to end the conflict than to fully satisfy your interests?

Do you think the other party might want to end the conflict rather than pushing for everything they wanted?

COLLABORATE

We collaborate by integrating interests and arriving at a solution that provides maximum satisfaction to all involved. Collaboration was identified as a style of conflict resolution consistent with integrative bargaining, but it can also be considered a way to use power — a way to affect the decisions, actions, and behavior of the other party.

Integrating your needs with the needs of the other party pays dividends, but you may ask: how do I collaborate when I can barely stomach having a conversation with the other party? In the heat of conflict, the idea of collaboration sounds preposterous. This is when your earlier work in addressing emotional upsets, communication breakdowns, false attributions, and overcoming other barriers pays off. Once you drain negative emotion, heal wounds, and repair broken communication, a renewed sense of purpose appears that fuels a desire to work jointly toward resolution.

Collaboration, however, does not usually spring from a sudden outpouring of brotherly love, but rather emerges as a conscious choice. Taking a collaborative approach is an act of will in which you move beyond hostility to join the other party on the same side of the table.

Collaboration may seem daunting, but sometimes it is the most effective use of power. When you collaborate, you orchestrate other types of power. When you seek to co-author the outcome, you change the conflict dynamics and generate the power needed to make things happen.

✎

What might prevent collaboration?

What guidelines will make collaboration possible?

Can you separate the people from the problem?

Do you need help finding creative approaches to negotiation?

NEGOTIATING THE USE OF POWER

When we think of negotiation, we think of back-and-forth dialogue regarding substantive outcomes. *Who will get what?* Equally important is negotiating the process, negotiating the procedures and guidelines to be used. Negotiation regarding procedure determines how parties will use their power during the process, which ultimately determines if they feel the process was fair and just.

Mediation satisfaction includes feeling good about *how* the outcome was achieved: you must feel the process was fair and just—you must experience *process or procedural satisfaction.*

In addition, you must experience *psychological satisfaction*: you must feel you were respected and that your feelings were honored. If you resolve the conflict but nonetheless feel you were treated unjustly or disrespectfully, or if you feel the process was unfair, you depart dissatisfied.

❦

Will you need to negotiate the use of power in mediation?

Will you need to hold coercive power in abeyance during mediation?

How do you typically use power to affect others? Does this generally result in your satisfying your interests?

Are the interests of the other party usually satisfied?

Will you need to change the way you use power to resolve this conflict?

TWENTY

Apology

IN THE SEARCH for reconciliation, the mediator begins to construct a metaphorical bridge between the parties. At first, he establishes a temporary bridge, then he facilitates construction of a bridge that will remain standing after his work is completed. Like a construction foreman, he helps parties locate building materials and provides a blueprint for a safe and secure bridge.

Parties begin to engage in the heavy lifting required to construct a lasting structure, but barriers materialize and block their path; impasse halts forward progress; construction stalls. Yet the work must continue, so the mediator guides the parties around emerging barriers.

Perhaps the most common barrier is a lack of apology. While extending an apology may seem simple, delivering an effective apology can be more demanding than a simple "I'm sorry." If we do not know how to construct and deliver a valid apology, we jeopardize our effort to construct a bridge to reconciliation.

~

Describe the role apology will play in the resolution of this dispute.

How might the mediator assist with the exchange of apologies?

THE VALUE OF AN APOLOGY

A carefully conceived apology imparts a medley of benefits; the more benefits delivered, the more likely the apology will be accepted. The following sections analyze the value of an apology.[1]

169

[Note: The terms *offender* and *victim* imply that one party has committed a harmful act and the other has been damaged, but this is rarely accurate — usually both parties have committed harmful acts and both have been harmed.]

APOLOGY SHOWS RESPECT

When you admit committing transgressions, you demonstrate humility; you lower yourself and lift the other up in a show of respect. Admitting misdeeds restores dignity to the person who has been diminished by harmful acts. When someone is harmed, they are robbed, intentionally or unintentionally, of pride and dignity. A harmful deed communicates that they are not valued. An apology restores their value. An apology reverses the victim's humiliation. It demonstrates the offender's willingness to also suffer shame and humiliation. An apology shifts focus from the offender's needs to the victim's needs.

Errors May Sabotage an Apology

Errors include all the ways we might fail to show respect. Apologies that are delivered with a superior attitude show disrespect. Apologies mumbled as an aside convey disrespect. Attempts to maintain a dominant or coercive position can undermine an apology. In order to convey respect, we must lift the other up, not keep them down.

During the course of a conflict, you may have come to perceive the other party as evil. The idea of humbling yourself before them creates emotions so strong they render you unable to act. Overwhelmed, you must first address your strong feelings in more depth. Was your attribution of evil incorrect? Must you now adjust your perceptions? Must you also apologize for your false attributions? Or have you hit a true impasse that demands another process?

❦

Will you be able to assume a humble attitude that conveys respect?

Will you be able to acknowledge that you caused harm?

Will you be able to solicit forgiveness?

Will it be possible to lift up the other?

Will false attributions inhibit your ability to apologize?

Empathetic Expressions of Concern

An apology tells the offended party that you feel their pain and suffering. It does not matter whether or not the harm they suffered was a direct result of your actions — your empathy shows that you understand their hurt, regardless of its cause.

If you fail to express empathy, the other party is not certain you truly "get it." If you do not demonstrate that you feel their hurt, they may fear you are so insensitive that you will cause them pain in the future. If empathy is missing, the victim doubts the wisdom of collaboration. On the other hand, a sincere apology that expresses empathy assures them you can see the world as they do — complete with hurt and humiliation. This sets the table for collaboration.

Possible errors include delivering a breezy, abstract, or glib apology that fails to connect with the hurt they feel. Such an apology will not convince them that you grasp the harm they suffered. It will seem you do not understand the severity of their pain. In contrast, an empathetic apology connects at a feeling level. It is not easily faked: counterfeit empathy sounds false and hollow.

A non-empathetic apology can block dialogue. The process grinds to a halt while the cause of impasse — lack of empathy — goes unrecognized. The victim strives harder to make the offender *feel their pain*. A similar but more egregious error takes place when the offender questions the victim's suffering and implies that the victim could not possibly suffer as much as they claim.

In summary, if you are unable to perceive the feelings of the other person and care about those feelings, your apology comes up short.

❦

Will you need to demonstrate empathy?

Will the other party need to show they care about the harm you suffered?

Is it possible that a lack of empathy has contributed to this conflict?

Do you feel you understand the suffering the other experienced?

Do you feel the other party has understood what you experienced?

Apology Expresses Acceptance of Responsibility

If you omit a statement of responsibility for your harmful acts, your sincerity is doubted. The other party worries that you will inflict additional harm, as you have not properly understood how past actions caused suffering. In the eyes of the other party, you are a continuing source of potential danger.

In contrast, if you accept responsibility, the other party gains comfort, as they see you are sufficiently cognizant of your actions to avoid future wrongdoing. When you take responsibility for harm done, you acknowledge that you possess the free will needed to control your actions. Implicitly, you promise to make better decisions in the future.

Errors include apologizing for the wrong action or apologizing for acts of little import, while neglecting important misdeeds. You undermine your apology when you deflect blame by attributing other cause to the harm you delivered. This becomes extreme when you deflect blame by implying that the victim caused their own suffering. Variations of deflection include blaming chance, nature, or even God for the misfortune that befell the victim.

If you claim your actions were the result of unknown forces, the apology falls short. An apology also fails when you promise you will take responsibility *if* the other party *also* takes responsibility. While most conflicts involve mutual responsibility, attempts to mitigate and diffuse blame weaken the apology.

Deflection provokes the harmed party to seek to penalize and punish you. The more unwilling you are to acknowledge responsibility, the more the victim wants to teach you a lesson. Yet it is difficult to accept responsibility for harm. We automatically shroud the memory of our misdeeds with a blanket of forgetting. We furiously rewrite the narrative to justify our behavior and script accounts that excuse our failings.

Thus, when the other party wants you to claim responsibility for your harmful deeds, you struggle. When you embrace your misdeed, other transgressions tumble into view and the task expands. One way to limit this cascade of regret is to ask the harmed party to describe specific acts that pained them. Though their analysis will probably differ from yours, their perception of your transgressions provides a starting point from which to structure an apology.

However, when your views do not match, you may want to focus your apology on those things you honestly perceive to be your responsibility. Though your apology may not be a perfect match with their grievances, the apology demonstrates a willingness to offer sincere remorse for events *as you see them*. This may not be ideal, but in many cases the other party, most of all, wants to see us struggle and come face-to-face with the person we are ashamed to be. This experience, they conclude, will make us much less likely to repeat harmful acts. They believe the distress we feel for having to account for our misdeeds will serve as a deterrent in the future.

❦

How will you express responsibility for events that transpired?

What will you need to hear from the other party regarding their responsibility?

Is it not yet clear who is responsible for events that transpired?

Is there cause for embarrassment that must be overcome?

Apology and the Moral Grain of the Universe

An apology should acknowledge the existence of a moral perspective and should acknowledge that wrongs committed violated moral foundations. Acknowledging morality sets the stage for a discussion of right and wrong — a foundation for future agreements.

Errors include expressions of regret detached from a moral perspective or expressions of regret that do not acknowledge free will. Those who will not acknowledge that they are free to make moral choices find it difficult to express regret. Victims are left doubting that moral concerns will guide the future actions of offenders. Victims worry the offender sees no value in compassion or caring.

The moral focus that concerns us is not a focus on the violation of rules as much as on the *violation of relationship*. The moral grain of the universe is relationship-based rather than rule-based. This does not mean we toss aside all agreements and rules, but rather that we judge morality in the context of relationship. Faced with an offender who does not recognize a moral perspective, we become concerned about the nature of our relationship, which may cause us to abandon mediation.

⤙

Will it be necessary to convey regret?

Do you hope to reestablish the damaged relationship?

Do you believe the other party feels regret?

Was the moral grain of the universe violated?

In what way have moral choices affected the relationship?

What will signal you can once again trust the other party?

Apology Signals Desire for Forgiveness

An apology may be a plea "to take away my guilt." In such cases, an offender expresses a desire to jettison his burden of guilt and cast off his identity as a wrongdoer. An apology may request help in transforming a harmful self into a repentant self worthy of being accepted back into a relationship. It communicates: "I need help to be made whole again." While this plea seems to focus on the offender's needs, the victim's dignity is boosted when the offender solicits help. Often the best compliment we can pay another is acknowledging the value of their help.

Errors include focusing so narrowly on your need for redemption that you exclude all concern for the harmed party. When your need to release a burden of guilt overshadows all thought of restitution, the apology seems self-serving. Balance is required. When an offender's focus on removing his guilt obscures his view of the victim's pain, the apology is compromised.

Miscues can be avoided by honoring the needs of the victim at the same time you unburden guilt: concern for absolution is balanced with concern for restitution. And yet the value a victim receives from your request for forgiveness should not be underestimated.

✑

Will it be necessary to ask for forgiveness?

Do you expect that the other party will ask you to forgive them?

Must a burden of guilt be set aside?

How will absolution and restitution be balanced?

Apology Expresses Willingness to Make Amends

An apology expresses willingness to deliver restitution or reparations. It sets the stage for the offender to make up damages. An expression of a desire to make the world right again restores relationship. The pledge to make restitution should be accompanied by a preliminary plan. Restitution may correct an imbalance directly, in a one-for-one manner. When intangibles such as reputation are lost, one might negotiate amends.

Errors include a failure to offer reparations or offering restitution to the wrong party. Restorative justice — in which offenders make amends to victims — attempts to remedy the error of restitution being made to the wrong party (the State). Other errors include failing to offer a realistic plan or failing to consult the victim when determining the appropriate restitution.

You might arrive at mediation prepared to make up damages, but during the back-and-forth of negotiation you may lose sight of your initial intention. You may grow weary and abandon the process. Thus, it pays to design a tentative plan that backs up an apology with an offer of reparation. The up-front willingness to negotiate in good faith goes a long way toward making the apology acceptable.

✐

Have you considered restitution? What must be done?

Will the other party need to make restitution?

How can the mediator help you assess damages?

Apology Signals a Desire to Reconcile

An apology signals a change of heart. It signals willingness to Restore Other Face. An apology communicates that the party feels the relationship is of sufficient value to warrant a humbling act of self-accusation.

The apology may offer a truce — a willingness to cease hostilities — or it may offer a concession: "you were right and I was wrong." You may concede that you did wrong in order to make it possible for the other party to Save Face and come to the table. In most cases, you hope for a reciprocal concession.

Errors include failing to make your desire for reconciliation clear. You might fail to ensure that the conciliatory nature of your message is understood. If the other party misreads your intention, they may become skeptical and seek to flush out an ulterior motive. This response may inadvertently challenge the sincerity of your apology. The victim does not appear to appreciate your goodwill gesture; they appear ungrateful, which prompts renewed hostility.

The party who apologizes should issue a disclaimer: they understand their apology may not end the conflict, but they have a personal need to change the tone of the conversation. They signal a clear change of heart as they offer to apologize in return for the other party listening closely. They propose exchanging their apology for respectful attention.

⤖

What role does Saving Face play in apology?

How might you offer a concession that signals willingness to change?

What concession might signal that the other party is serious about working with you?

How will you offer and recognize true concessions that will help bring reconciliation?

Apology Removes the Insult from the Injury

We hurt from the injury we suffer, but we also hurt from damaged pride. Insult becomes tangled up in injury. Thus, an apology must Restore Face to those insulted.

Errors stem from failures to recognize psychological needs. We may *fix the deal* gone awry but fail to *fix the person*. We are slow to recognize that emotional damage requires healing. We assume that the substance of the deal is paramount. Yet the contested deal may turn out to be minor, while the emotional pain suffered looms large.

An apology that ignores the insult delivered is invalid. This is common as most victims avoid admitting they suffered insult. If they admit they were hurt, they concede that they were vulnerable, and thus they Lose Face. For this reason, victims sequester their emotions and make it difficult for offenders to recognize the prior Face Loss that must be addressed.

To avoid this error, you can ask if your actions have given insult: "I have reason to believe I insulted you. Am I right?" This conveys that you are willing to hear the victim express grievances. In most instances, however, a victim would rather not confess weakness, so you should offer a blanket apology: "I realize what I did must have caused you pain. I cannot imagine how you felt, but I know it cannot have been pleasant. I wish to say I am sorry for causing any discomfort you might have experienced." Victims appreciate this type of apology as it frees them from the need to admit weakness or vulnerability.

❦

In this conflict, has insult been given?

What will need to be done to address past insults?

Will it be necessary for you to Save Face?

How might the need to Save Face affect your willingness to accept an apology?

Will it be necessary to Restore Face for the other party?

What will signal that the other party cares about your feelings?

Apology Promises the Harm Will Not Be Repeated

The offender vows that he will not repeat the transgression. The quality of the apology enables a victim to distinguish between an uncaring sociopath and a remorseful offender. The person who injures us and does not care is dangerous; such a sociopath, unable to feel the pain he caused, is likely to hurt us again. Sociopaths and narcissists have a tough time understanding why they should apologize; they find delivering a valid apology difficult, if not impossible. In contrast, people of good will want to apologize.

A victim does not feel safe until they know the offender's true intentions. In the past, they failed to recognize danger, so now they are more discerning and want to know the nature of the person with whom they are dealing.

Errors include promising that harmful actions will not be repeated — even though the current conflict arose because harmful behavior was repeated. The victim wonders — if change did not take place previously, why should he now expect a change? Why should he believe that promise? The apology must offer a credible plan for terminating harmful behavior.

The apology can fall short if the offender underestimates how difficult it will be to change. Most of us recognize that change is not easy; we acknowledge the difficulty. An apology can be improved by adding a realistic expression of the difficulty one expects to encounter. Perhaps proof of current attempts to change can be offered. Or one might express willingness to accept stiff penalties for future violations. The challenge we face is making sure our presentation does not inadvertently appear insincere or glib.

❦

How will you reassure the other party that harm will not be repeated?

What will you need to hear to reassure you that you will not be harmed again?

How difficult will it be to make changes that prevent the conflict from repeating?

What will need to happen for you to feel the other party will not repeat the harm done?

Apology Acknowledges Free Will

When an offender expresses conscious awareness of his choices — when he knows he possesses free will — he reassures his victim. If the apology does not reflect his ability to exercise choice, it is unlikely he can master his future decisions and behavior. The party that considers that events "just happen" has a difficult time convincing others that harmful acts will not be repeated.

Errors include offering an apology motivated by duress. If an apology is not freely given, the victim worries that harmful acts will be repeated. They worry the person does not really wish to apologize and is only satisfying the demand of someone with power. In contrast, a valid apology is an act of free will issuing from a person's heart.

What will you need to hear to know that the other party can exercise sufficient control to prevent further conflict?

Is there any reason to believe a party is not taking part in mediation voluntarily?

What will signal to the other party that you are in control of your actions?

An Apology Explains Why Things Happened

A detailed account provides the victim with clues that explain why events happened; clarification reduces uncertainty and gives the victim a better grasp on reality. A person harmed by another experiences a feeling of unreality. Rarely do we conceive ourselves to be a valid target of harmful deeds. Thus, when another harms us, we become confused and disoriented. The experience of being harmed seems unreal.

A clear explanation of why harmful acts took place helps the victim recover, as knowing *why* an offender caused harm dispels mystery. It is possible the transgression had nothing to do with the victim. With an accurate account in hand, the victim can discard false scenarios they created in their imagination, scenarios that often include self-doubt.

Errors occur when the explanation is unclear or illogical. A lack of clarity deepens rather than dispels the mystery. An explanation that lacks sufficient detail reflects a lack of introspection; it signals that the offender needs to achieve a better understanding of their actions.

It is common for offenders to attempt to Save Face with an account that veers into justification and deflects blame. Apologies heavy on justification and denial, however, do not explain misdeeds, but rather explain them away. It is particularly important for the offender to clarify his previous acts of deception, as this allows the victim to put events into a proper perspective.

To avoid these errors, make sure you can describe the causes of your actions in a clear manner. Consider whether or not your explanation contains sufficient detail. Does your account bring clarity? If the explanation avoids accounting for actual events, your narrative may warrant a deeper look. Ask yourself what information the other party will need in order to bring understanding and closure.

If the apology becomes a laundry list of reasons you should *not* be held accountable, it will fail. Taking full responsibility for at least one aspect of harm done is better than a long, self-excusing narrative.

Have you done a thorough assessment?

Can you explain why events happened as they did?

What about this conflict has been most confusing?

What is still not clear to you regarding this conflict?

Has something been hidden?

Apology Promotes Spiritual Growth

When your actions cause you dissatisfaction, when you feel disconnected and alienated from your true nature, you seek to transform your life. You embrace humility, which is paradoxically uplifting. When you bend low to apologize, you are lifted up. As you confront *"who you are not"* you gain insight into *"who you can be."*

When you offer an apology, the other party may or may not forgive you, but you nonetheless take the first step toward personal renewal. When you contemplate repentance, your thoughts may become shrouded in shadow, but with apology you begin a journey into the light. When you become mired in contemplating the darkness of your misdeeds, you miss the transformative power of an apology—a transformation that wipes away the residue of wrongdoing that obscures your true self. With an apology, you clean the mirror and experience uplifting renewal.

Errors include not endowing an apology with the respect it deserves. A glib and perfunctory apology does not flow from your heart. If you see apology as a degrading act of submission, you will not be lifted up. If you consider apology proof of how wicked and evil you are, rather than a gesture of rising above your flawed nature, you fail to realize its potential.

To overcome these errors, refuse the temptation to toss off a glib apology. Seek the deeper meaning of apology as part of a healing process and strive to transform shortcomings into wisdom.

How important is it to make peace?

Is there a need for improved spiritual awareness?

What wisdom has been missing?

Apology Provides an Opportunity for Confession

Parties may offer confessions during mediation. The need for such unburdening usually arrives unexpectedly. Previously, there was no one who could hear their story and accept their contrition without judgment, so they kept their personal narrative locked inside, waiting for the right moment. That may happen during mediation.

Confessions delivered privately to the mediator are not apologies; nonetheless, such confessions may be framed into an apology. The private unburdening often causes a dramatic change of demeanor. The other party may sense the presence of a new heart. The change can be so dramatic that the other party recognizes you have transformed your life. They often accept the change as proof that a renewal of relationship can take place.

Errors include missing the exact moment when it is safe to unburden. A party actively looking for an opportunity continually evaluates the mediator's ability to listen without judgment. They continually assess whether or not they trust the mediator. They may test the mediator as a prelude to unburdening and requesting help in structuring an apology.

Do you expect that a confession of wrongdoing will be an important aspect of reconciliation?

Is there anything important you must tell the other party so they will truly understand you?

Will you need to open your heart to hear the other party explain the challenges they face?

Will unburdening play a role in the resolution of this conflict?

Summary

Apologies can help us overcome impasse. Apology can reestablish respect and dignity and bring emotional tranquility. From a negotiation perspective, apology moves us toward a realistic appraisal of the restitution required and insures a more enduring settlement.

As you prepare an apology, should one be needed, make sure to deliver all the value possible. Delivering an apology is not easy; only a careful and considered approach moves us toward reconciliation. Likewise, should you expect to receive an apology, consider how that other party's apology will satisfy your needs.

What challenges might occur with respect to apology?

How might the mediator best help you?

PARTIALLY HIDDEN GUILT

An offender may suffer a painful form of guilt when they are uncertain whether or not the victim knows they are responsible for harmful acts. The offender may assume their actions were hidden and remain unknown but, at the same time, they may fear their misdeeds have been secretly discovered. They are trapped, wondering whether or not the other party knows the exact nature of their harmful actions. The offender's thoughts alternate between "they must have found out" and "they could not possibly have found out." The anxiety is brutally taxing, causing them to become erratic, alternating between hostility and propitiation. Mood swings become extreme.

Thus, if the other party accuses you of wrongdoing with anger that seems unrealistic and if their accusations lack logic, there is a high probability they suffer uncertainty as to whether or not *you* discovered *their* misdeeds.

Litigation, with its adversarial discovery phase, exacerbates this phenomenon. Litigants worry and wonder: *what do they really know? What remains hidden?* When a client is advised by their attorney to be less than forthcoming at the same time the opposing attorney seeks to expose their dishonesty, the client experiences brutal uncertainty that leads to anxiety-driven anger.

One way to deescalate the problem is to be forthright in stating what you know and do not know. Reveal your concerns about the other party's behavior. You may say, "I don't know what you think I might know, but here are the issues about which I have concern." Or, "I know you have committed (specific misdeeds) and I am willing to discuss how that affected me — if that is important to you." Or, "I know it can be very uncomfortable to not know what someone else knows about you. If there is anything you need to tell me, I will listen." Or take the mediator aside and tell him you suspect the other party has not disclosed transgressions that weigh on their conscience and they may need an opportunity to meet privately to clear the air. The mediator may say to the upset and angry party, "Sometimes things we have not told the other party cause discomfort. If this is a concern, let me know and we can discuss it." This may bring considerable relief.

❦

Are there things you would rather the other party not find out?

Is there confusion regarding what the other party knows or does not know?

Do you sense the other party is worried about what you know or don't know?

How will you signal that you are willing to listen to an apology?

WHY PEOPLE DO NOT APOLOGIZE

When we apologize, we move through our fear, relieve feelings of guilt and shame, change the terms of negotiation, and increase the odds we will reconcile. There is no quick and easy or painless way to accomplish these steps; as a result, some parties balk when it comes to apology.

While a mediator hopes to guide the mediation process to reconciliation, some parties simply wish to cut a deal and move on. They seek the fastest way of disentangling from the other party. This outcome does not seek to improve relationship; rather, the mediator facilitates a resolution that satisfies immediate needs. He may then suggest parties re-engage at a later date to work on healing the relationship.

A party may avoid offering an apology if they anticipate that their self-image will suffer irreparable harm. They may fear the other party will think less of them and terminate the relationship. They find it difficult to imagine their apology will garner forgiveness; instead, they expect retaliation. They do not see compassion as a possible response.

In addition, an attorney may advise a client against making an apology, fearing the content will be used in court as an admission of guilt. While this concern has some validity, there are safe methods of apologizing in the legal setting. Mediation confidentiality may apply or your attorney may construct an apology that navigates past unwanted legal exposure. For more on this approach, consult "Advising Clients to Apologize."[2]

When an abusive opposing party views our apology as a weakness to be exploited, we may legitimately decide to withhold apology. This fear is usually overblown, but if the mediator senses danger as well, it may be best to postpone apology. For example, in cases involving an abusive spouse, ending abuse takes precedence over apology. In the special case of abuse, skilled professionals should guide the process.

An obsessive *need to be right* may offset the desire to apologize. Admitting we were wrong may make us feel our survival is threatened. Such an obsessive need to be right may block a party's ability to articulate their misgivings regarding apology. Their emotions may block their ability to look inward. In order to address the *must-be-right* barrier, the party may need adequate time to sit with a counselor and explore their emotions.

When mediation stalls as a result of impasse, it pays to consider an apology — in spite of the challenges involved. It is one tool that can revitalize the process and allow parties to move forward.

&

In this mediation, do you wish to reach an agreement and move on?

Will you need to work with your attorney on a "safe apology"?

Is physical, verbal, or emotional abuse a factor?

Discuss potential abuse with your attorney and the mediator.

In this conflict, is there a concern over who is right and who is wrong?

TWENTY-ONE

Forgiveness

FORGIVENESS MAY BE the most elusive step in reconciliation. You might ask, must we forgive in order to resolve a conflict? Is forgiveness absolutely necessary?

It is possible to *resolve* a conflict without forgiveness. You may settle a dispute without extending forgiveness. Each party goes their separate way. However, if you desire the fruits of a restored relationship, if you desire *reconciliation*, you will need to consider forgiveness.

FORGIVENESS IS NOT CONTINGENT ON APOLOGY

An apology can be offered regardless of whether or not forgiveness is extended. Likewise, forgiveness is not contingent on an apology. We can forgive even when another refuses to apologize. Often, however, apology and forgiveness are linked: a heartfelt apology frequently prompts forgiveness.

Reciprocity plays an additional role in forgiveness. As we struggle to forgive, we may recognize our need *to be forgiven*, which makes us hesitant *not* to forgive the other. We worry that if we refuse to forgive, we risk being turned away when *we* need forgiveness.

The idea that we might need to reciprocate, however, only serves to give us pause. Such fear-based motivation will not inspire forgiveness, for we forgive, not from weakness or fear, but rather from a compassionate desire to bestow a gift on the other.

⚬

Will you be able to extend forgiveness to another who refuses to apologize?

Will you be able to give that which has not been earned?

Will you be able to freely give the gift of forgiveness?

BARRIERS TO FORGIVING

Retribution and revenge generate such strong adversity that we turn away from those options — but we never totally abandon the desire to get even. We may set aside the immediate urge to exact revenge, but at a barely conscious level, we remain invested in the possibility of retribution. As we try to forgive, this desire resurfaces: retributive scenarios haunt our daydreams. An inner voice whispers, "return the blow and make them pay." We discover just how difficult it is to abandon the thirst for revenge.

Or you may turn away and refuse to acknowledge the other's existence. Perhaps you cannot obliterate them physically, but you vow to obliterate them from your mind. For you the offender no longer exists: he or she becomes a non-person. However, this method rarely works. Uninvited ghostly images of the offender appear in your mind and disturb your peace. To escape, you shutter your consciousness with drugs, alcohol, or the stupor of depression. Ironically, your attempt to "disappear" the offender precipitates your own disappearance. Your diminished consciousness becomes a barrier to your happiness.

Or you may convert your wounded status into victimhood. You display your wounds as symbols of identity — as a victim. You invite the world to know you by your wounds. You cling to your victim identity, which has become valuable just as a crutch is valuable to an injured man. Intuitively, you realize forgiving means you must set aside and abandon any public display of your wounds. But all too often you are unwilling to jettison the victim identity you carefully crafted.

What decisions have you made that make it more difficult for you to forgive the other party?

What factors might inhibit your ability to forgive?

DISMANTLING BARRIERS

Handling the Revenge Impulse

As the pain of injury or injustice lingers, the revenge impulse resurfaces. Although the impulse may appear logical and sane, you know that revenge brings adversity — not peace and contentment.

Dismantling the urge takes time and repeated efforts. When thoughts of revenge surface, you must greet hot emotion with cold logic. You must consider the costs of vengeance. While you can accept and acknowledge the revenge urge as natural, even expected, you must then dismantle the urge with rational analysis.

You assume revenge will satisfy the need to make the other party experience the pain you *felt*. But then you must consider that it will: (a) leave you struggling with guilt for the pain you *cause*, (b) result in lowered self-esteem after you dispense injury or harm, and (c) result in remorse as you watch the other party stagger from physical, emotional, or mental wounds you deliver.

You add up the costs and wonder if the burdens — guilt, loss of self-esteem, and remorse — are too heavy. You may anticipate that, as your anger subsides, you will realize what you *really* desired was your own happiness — not the other's suffering. While you may dream that their suffering will translate into your happiness, you know deep down it is highly unlikely that retribution will deliver genuine happiness.

This analysis supplies a warning — once we engage in revenge, we risk sliding into chronic hatred. It is not only *our* hatred we must anticipate; revenge leads to reciprocal retaliation. Scripted Hollywood drama may satisfy a need to see the scales of justice balanced with acts of revenge, but we know this is rarely possible, as the other party does not view our attempt to balance the scales in the same light we do. Individuals inevitably value their own hurt as more costly than the hurt another suffers. From their viewpoint, they are justified in settling the score anew. Their focus turns to making *us* pay a price.

The strength of the revenge impulse may convince you to set aside your rational cost analysis. You may argue that revenge is meant to teach the wrongdoer a lesson — exacting revenge becomes altruistic and worthy of your sacrifice. Retributive punishment, however, rarely educates anyone: pain, suffering, and degradation do not fuel insight. As a general rule, pain and suffering *diminish* awareness. Pain teaches us to react rather than reason. Pain renders us dumber not wiser.

People consumed with pain act while in a stupor. The long-term result is a less-aware culture, a people confused about what matters, a people acting from a state of semi-consciousness.

&

In this conflict, have you wanted to take revenge?

If you took revenge, what would be the consequences?

Would you like to see the other party punished for their part in this conflict?

Do you feel you might be the target of the other party's need for revenge?

What help will you need from the mediator to move past the need for revenge?

Diminished Consciousness

Banishing the offender from your mind might seem a likely path to contentment and happiness. Rarely, however, are we able to erase the offender and their harmful acts from our consciousness. Wounds frozen into mental images take on a life of their own; memories encysted with negative emotions are triggered when we encounter the offender. Our overall ability to respond to life with enthusiasm, caring and love is diminished.

During conflict resolution, negative emotions once buried are triggered. Painful memories block the ability to forgive and prevent healing. When people decide to banish the hurt from their minds, they often pursue diminished consciousness through drink or drugs, or they retreat into the stupor of depression. Unconsciousness, however, never actually erases pain and suffering: it simply clouds reality. It drapes an imaginary black veil over upsets people do not wish to view. The shrouded pain, however, continues to exist—hidden behind the curtain. Diminished consciousness causes wounds to fester and releases poisons that make people ill.

As you move toward forgiveness, you may need to overcome the negative effects of diminished consciousness. In order to heal, you must bring truthfulness and specificity to your forgiveness. Truthfulness calls for "harmony between the message you give to the outside world and the feelings you keep on the inside."[1] Forgiveness demands full awareness, as when you forgive, you forgive with specificity.

Have you sought to get the other party out of your mind?

What strategies have you used to cope with the discomfort of this conflict?

What problems arose when you tried to push this dispute out of your mind?

Do you anticipate that it will be difficult for the other party to sit in front of you?

What might the mediator do to make it possible to be in the same room?

What valuable information might you have missed?

Victim Identity

If you take on the role of a victim, you wear your wounds as a badge, rather than diminishing their hold over you. Others may sympathize initially, but eventually they lose interest and treat you like the victim you claim to be. This victim role may be extremely difficult to shed if it accrues significant value.

You may implicitly label your offender as evil through your public victim status, which exacts the revenge of negative public opinion. Your ability to publicly shame your offender has value you may be reluctant to abandon. You may realize that if you forgive, you must forfeit the value you derive from the public display of victimhood.

Dismantling this barrier requires an honest assessment of the actual benefit you derive — are you purchasing freedom and happiness or are you inadvertently purchasing bondage?

❦

Are you seen as a victim in this conflict?

Has the other party been viewed as a victim?

Who have you talked to about the hurt you suffered?

Do you feel the other party wants you to admit you harmed them?

Should more people know about the harm the other party did?

What might you have to give up in order to forgive?

Fairness

One additional barrier warrants special attention: concern with fairness. We are deeply offended when our attempt to even the score leads to adverse consequences *for us*. When attempts to make things right cause *us* to suffer, life seems terribly unfair. We become bitter and unwilling to consider forgiveness at such a high price. Though we consider forgiving, we see only injustice.

If you fight back, you become stuck to the evil you fight, like a fly on flypaper. In your attempts to destroy your opponent, you become even more firmly chained to them. Thus, in conflict, the solution you *really* seek is different than you might imagine — the outcome you seek is *to no longer be stuck*. The goal is to be free — to no longer be held captive in the oppositional embrace. However, when you lash out you become chained to that which you seek to destroy; you are dragged into life's quicksand.

After crashing into the consequences of striking back, you may decide to explore overlooked options, such as forgiveness. Forgiveness neuters your strike-back impulse: you must forego dreams of extracting an eye for an eye. But you may wonder, how fair or just is a world that does not allow you to strike a return blow? There are no easy answers, and no quick solutions. As you consider forgiveness, you may need to make sure that your protest against unfairness or injustice does not block your path to reconciliation and happiness.

✥

Do you feel a strong need to defeat evil?

Do you consider that forgiveness is unfair?

Does the other party have anything to gain by keeping you tangled up in conflict?

Does the other party want to control you by keeping you embroiled in conflict?

Does the other party consider that you have committed evil acts?

Will you continue to harbor resentment even after you forgive? How will you get past that burden?

FORGIVENESS DEFINED

Forgiving another for the hurt they have inflicted does not occur magically or fortuitously. It is not a warm fuzzy feeling arising mysteriously from the distant shores of our psyche. *Forgiveness is an act of the will.*

You must actively decide to forgive those who inflicted harm you did not deserve. Forgiveness is not something you owe: the party who hurt you does not deserve your forgiveness. Forgiveness does not right the scales of justice or balance wrongs; it is not a *quid pro quo*. Rather, forgiveness is an affirmative act of compassion that disregards balancing scales and tallying debts. While revenge tries to even the score, forgiveness tears up the scorecard.

When you are harmed, you experience being made less. With revenge you seek to make the offender less — physically, emotionally, and mentally. In contrast, when you forgive *you lift the offender up* and make *more* of him. In spite of your hurt and your loss, you increase the compassion and love in the world; you lessen suffering and increase peace, happiness and contentment.

An exercise of free will summons forgiveness. It requires humility and demands that you release control over the other. When you forgive, you accept the other *as they are*, including their flaws and shortcomings. Forgiving requires a compassion that allows you to relinquish the power used to exact consequences.

Forgiveness is not a cowardly alternative to vengeance; forgiveness defiantly affirms a different reality. In choosing forgiveness you dramatically decide to change yourself, the other, the relationship, and the world. Forgiving is not a passive event. It is an act of will.

❧

Recall a time when the forgiveness you needed was refused.

Recall a time when you were forgiven.

What is most important about forgiveness?

Will forgiving the other party allow you to put down a burden and move on?

ABILITY TO FORGIVE

When you first decide to forgive, you suffer doubt: you are not certain you are capable of forgiving. You feel you are being asked to go out on a ledge and jump. However, forgiveness sets in motion a transformation and bestows ability you previously lacked. The *decision* transforms you: after you jump, you grow wings. The act of will summons latent ability where, previously, doubts ruled. To forgive is paradoxical, counterintuitive, illogical, and difficult to comprehend. But your decision to forgive propels you past doubt.

❧

Do you worry you will not be able to forgive?

Is there a part of you that refuses to forgive?

Is there a part of you that wants to forgive?

Do you believe it is possible for the other party to forgive?

What might allow you to risk considering forgiveness?

SELF-FORGIVENESS

When you cannot forgive self, it is nearly impossible to forgive another. The reason for this may seem puzzling and counterintuitive — the anger you feel toward another most often has its roots in *your own transgressions*. We incorrectly assume an angry person must have been harmed — *that's why they are angry*. We witness their anger and assume they suffered at the hands of the person they target with their anger.

Ironically, harmful acts *we committed* often cause our anger toward others. This idea may seem strange or even offensive, but it rests on observations you can verify. Consider the following explanation:

When we commit a misdeed, our self-image suffers. When we harm others, we find it difficult to accept our actions, as we do not see ourselves as bad or evil. We battle to maintain a positive identity, but our commission of harmful acts threatens self-image. To maintain positive self-image — after harming another — we alter (in our memory) the sequence of events. We write a story consistent with the self-image we wish to maintain. We mask our narrative duplicity with a reality-blurring storm of disturbed emotions. We redraft events to bolster our desired self-image.

To preserve self-worth, we argue that the person we harmed *deserved* harm — *they had it coming*. We attribute evil nature to them — which justifies our causing them harm. In our emotionally blurred memory, time becomes inverted. The harm the other allegedly committed is conceived to have happened *before* we harmed them. Our misdeeds are flipped in our mind and become reciprocal actions taken to punish another who deserved punishment.

If a sleight-of-hand time shift is not possible, we concoct a preemptive-strike rationale. We claim that we detected their harmful intention, which justified punishing them *before* they did harm. In rewriting our narrative — to protect our "white hat" identity — we create the other party as a villain worthy of our anger and harmful acts. Our anger ratchets upward in direct relationship to how badly we harmed those against whom we complain. We offset guilt with tales of wrong done *to us*; the greater the harm we caused, the more we must justify our anger.

Altered inner narratives protect us from recognizing our flaws. Unfortunately, when we cannot admit our harmful acts, we also cannot forgive. We hold the false narrative in place and remain angry. Forgiveness is blocked, for if we forgive the other and remove them from the category of evildoer, the house of cards we built might crumble. We might expose an aspect of self we do not wish to see. Thus, to protect self-image, we continue to demonize the other. The self we hide is in need of forgiveness, but lacking self-forgiveness, we are trapped. We become a chronically angry person.

On the other hand, if we admit that we, too, are flawed and in need of forgiveness, if we acknowledge our imperfect nature and engage in self-forgiveness, the impasse is broken. Self-forgiveness, we discover, is a prerequisite to forgiving the other.

The angry party, after unburdening and finding self-forgiveness, may admit, "I realize I've not been an angel either. I need to apologize for a few things myself..." They engage in reciprocal apology. Both admit wrongdoing. Reciprocal apology often implies forgiveness: "Your transgressions are offset by my understanding that I have also done harm." Mutual forgiveness emerges. A mediator must pay close attention: such forgiveness often takes place nonverbally during acknowledgement of mutual culpability.

In summary, when the moment to forgive arrives, if you find only anger and hatred in your heart, inspect your conscience. Do you need forgiveness? Has self-forgiveness been missing?

It is difficult to achieve reconciliation if one suffers from a troubled heart that has not been forgiven. There is benefit to be gained from a period of solitude, during which you spend time inspecting your conscience. This is not easy. Unraveling transgressions is tough work. We prefer to wear the "white hat" while blaming the other; therefore, we convince ourselves that there is no reason to dig up old bones. However, even though soul searching may be uncomfortable, the short-term pain is less than the pain of unresolved conflict.

In this conflict, did anything happen you wish had not happen? Anything you regret?

Do you need forgiveness to end this conflict?

Is it easy for you to forgive yourself? Are you more likely to excuse yourself than to forgive yourself?

Does confessing and asking for forgiveness have benefit to you?

Does your attention return over and over to something you might have done wrong in this conflict? What would it feel like to be free of that burden?

What would you most like to "do over" when it comes to this dispute?

TWENTY-TWO

Impasse

PARTIES MAY REACH a resolution but stop short of reconciliation; or they may end the process without resolution and seek a verdict from a judge, jury, or elder. They may take matters into their own hands. Failure to achieve reconciliation stems from an inability to move beyond impasse.

Throughout the process, the mediator avoids imposing a settlement outcome and is aware that not all attempts to mediate end in success. When further effort appears futile, she does not fault the parties; instead, she seeks to identify impediments causing impasse. She reminds participants that significant gains often emerge from the daunting challenge of overcoming seemingly intractable barriers.

Perhaps the most prevalent barrier is the hidden influence of a destructive third party, the antithesis of a mediator. Unlike the mediator, the destructive party is invested in keeping conflict alive. This barrier—the destructive hidden influence—is often not readily visible; thus, we tend to overlook its presence. When the reason for impasse becomes puzzling, assess the situation and search for signs of a destructive hidden influence, a third party that seeks to keep the conflict alive.

❧

Has impasse blocked the path to a negotiated resolution?

Has the hope of reconciliation slipped away?

How would you describe the impediments to reconciliation?

Who might want the conflict to continue?

THE DESTRUCTIVE HIDDEN INFLUENCE

The destructive hidden influence, the covert third party, is the antithesis of the mediator who acts as a *constructive third party*. The mediator helps parties resolve conflict, while the destructive third party covertly promotes conflict.

A mediator helps parties:

- identify and remedy miscommunication and misunderstanding;

- identify interests and motivations;

- design creative solutions that satisfy interests through collaboration;

- heal the hurt suffered;

- recognize and admit transgressions;

- structure and deliver apologies;

- find their forgiving heart;

- extend forgiveness to those who caused harm;

- plan for a future based on mutual caring;

- help parties and attorneys draft guidelines or settlement agreements;

- acknowledge reconciliation through ritual.

The mediator seeks transparency and full disclosure. He or she nurtures active participation and party self-determinism. In contrast, the destructive third party:

- intentionally creates miscommunication and misunderstanding;

- causes confusion regarding interests and motivations;

- defeats attempts at collaboration;

- exacerbates pain and suffering;

- discourages and sabotages apology and forgiveness;

- actively blocks reconciliation efforts.

The destructive hidden influence strives to defeat self-determinism and seeks to impose covert control over others. He avoids transparency, choosing instead to operate in the shadows and foment conflict. He is the covert agent keeping the fight going.

All conflict is the result, to a greater or lesser degree, of such destructive hidden influences. An old saying claims that it takes two to tangle. But, in reality, it takes three to fight: the two parties overtly engaged in conflict and a covert or hidden third party. The hidden nature of the destructive third party causes conflicts to rage even when the warring parties wish to end hostility. The covert agent's invisibility introduces mystery and confusion.

In long-running conflicts, the influence of the destructive third party becomes buried under subsequent hostilities, making it difficult to discover their initial role. Your attention fixates on the other party's hostile acts while the destructive person fades into the background and becomes a *hidden influence*. You see only your adversary and your adversary sees only you; both miss the actual cause of the fight.

The conflict escalates as the hidden influence plants and nurtures false attributions. Years later, parties find it difficult, nearly impossible, to recognize the actual underlying cause of conflict. They both recall being the target of hostility from the other party; their memories support their previously voiced complaints about the other. But the real cause, the hidden influence, has remained obscured. Considerable effort is required to guide disputants through the maze of hostility to locate the original cause of their mutual antipathy.

These dynamics play out whether the conflict is a family matter, an office quarrel, a business dispute, a public policy dispute, or a clash between nations. A skilled mediator employs calm persistence, insight, diligence, acute perception, and considerable skill to uncover these hidden influences — the offstage third parties covertly driving conflict.

A mediator queries parties about the sources of information that contributed to their views. Who helped form their opinion of the other party? She poses questions that expose sources of negative or alarming information. She tracks down sources of disparaging opinions. She sorts through a roster of people with influence: friends, acquaintances, co-workers, associates and others.

With a casual demeanor, she queries: "Who will benefit if you continue to fight?" Parties rarely recognize the subtle psychological benefits a destructive hidden influence enjoys when others battle. For example, a boss embroiled in constant conflict with Office Worker A does not notice the sub-standard work of Office Worker B. This benefits B (who covertly fuels the fight).

In another example, two siblings battle constantly. They fail to notice that their mother covertly fuels their conflict. The sibling's spats deflect attention that might otherwise be directed to the mother and her shortcomings.

In a similar scenario, two nations at war are no longer able to devote resources to compete with a third nation — the hidden destructive influence covertly promoting their conflict. The third nation secretly benefits from the war they fomented behind the scenes.

As a party to a conflict, you will want to assess who would be threatened if you reconciled. Who has the most to lose if the relationship is healed and friendship restored? Who might feel excluded? Who might lose status? Who may no longer be a source of inside information? Gentle probing uncovers the previously overlooked hidden influence.

When you identify the destructive hidden influence, the conflict resolves quickly. You recall times you became distrustful — because of a whispered secret, a dropped hint, or damaging innuendo. The conflict subsequently unravels with amazing speed.

Who have you relied on for information or advice regarding the other party?

List friends, associates and acquaintances you have in common with the other party.

Who will benefit if you fail to resolve this conflict?

Who has pointed out the other party's flaws and shortcomings?

Do you need to avoid becoming a victim of the other party's flaws or shortcomings?

Has someone pointed out your flaws and shortcomings?

What does the other party do that annoys people?

How do you know the other party annoys people?

How will you encourage the other party to disclose what others have said about you?

HIDDEN INFLUENCES DRIVEN BY FEAR

The destructive hidden influence, the offstage third party, can be found in every walk of life and at every level of society. They are driven by fear-based paranoia: they fear becoming an outcast if others enjoy loving relationships. They perceive another's happiness as a threat. The young lady who feels insecure pits her friends against each other, covertly defending herself against being ostracized. She reduces the perceived threat by entangling others in conflict. In her mind, if friends distrust one another, she benefits from increased attention. Conversely, if they enjoy a close relationship, she might be abandoned.

The chronically destructive party experiences constant fear: in their mind, everyone seeks to destroy them. This pathological fear drives every action. As long as others are kept off balance, the destructive person feels safe. They work diligently to prevent discovery of their covert and manipulative activity.

Most people cannot begin to imagine fear so irrational. Such extreme and pervasive fear makes no sense. This makes the destructive hidden influence difficult to recognize—in large measure they are invisible because the mental state behind their actions is hard to believe.

Fortunately, the number afflicted with such all-consuming fear is small; unfortunately, the destruction they cause can be significant. We all experience bouts of fear-based insecurity, but such bouts do not compare with the pathological destructive third party driven to compulsively destroy relationships. They must constantly undermine others with ongoing destructive counter-measures.

Perhaps one reason that mediation resolves conflict lies with a mediator's role as a *positive* third party, which stands in counterpoint to the *negative* third party covertly active in most conflicts. The antidote to a destructive third party is a constructive third party. Whereas the hidden destructive third party keeps parties at one another's throats, the constructive third party helps them reconcile.

In some cases, the destructive hidden influence may pretend to mediate a dispute while covertly making things worse. In their hands, it may appear mediation does not work. We must be aware that a destructive party may masquerade as a peacemaker. They may sabotage the group's handling of internal disputes.

The other liability that arises when associates take on the role of a mediator is their inability to identify the destructive third party. They find it difficult to root out hidden influences, as the destructive party's covert influence extends throughout the group. Thus, an in-house mediator may suffer blind spots as a result of third-party influence.

An impartial outside mediator creates trust. Then parties slowly become willing to "pull strings" to identify the hidden influence. As they become invested in finding a solution to the conflict, they cease protecting sources that have previously sworn them to secrecy. When they recognize the duplicitous role of the hidden influence, they reveal sources of gossip, character assassination, or covert dissent to the mediator.

After the hidden influence is exposed and revealed, antipathy between parties vanishes. They may share mutual embarrassment at having been duped; they may express regret at having accepted secretive negative views without allowing each other to defend themselves. Most of all, they no longer see gossip and character assassination in the same light.

In this conflict, is someone afraid others will get ahead?

If you reconcile with the other party, will anyone feel left out?

Is anyone jealous of your relationship with the other party?

If you reconcile, will anyone lose status?

Do you rely on inside sources of information?

How will you uncover back-channel communications?

How will you convince the other party to reveal hidden information?

Has anyone engaged in character assassination?

Has anyone attempted to ruin your reputation?

Has anyone advised against mediation? Who?

Has anyone told the other party that they should not trust you?

WALKING AWAY

When we have encountered a fear-driven destructive party and have become entangled in a situation beyond our personal ability to transform, we may choose to walk away, wiser for the experience. This option may seem to be little more than surrender and defeat. Nonetheless, the outcome is not entirely negative: we walk away having learned vital lessons that will serve us in the future. We have an opportunity to inspect how our decisions led to entanglement in a no-win situation.

When we analyze our behavior, we may recognize that we had misgivings; intuition warned us to avoid involvement, but we ignored the warning. When we accurately assess personal responsibility, we realize that events would not have taken place without our complicity. Our failing may have been as simple as paying too little attention or as significant as compromising our values. We learn from experience how to avoid those situations; we acquire increased ability to perceive trouble that inevitably leads to intractable conflict.

❧

Are you able to show compassion in the face of destructive intentions?

How will you determine if this conflict is beyond your ability to handle?

How can you take responsibility for the condition in which you find yourself?

Is it possible you could have avoided this conflict?

What role did you play in becoming entangled in this conflict?

WHEN WE CANNOT WALK AWAY

There are times when we cannot walk away; the destructive person continues to stalk us. It may appear that only raw force will extricate us from the situation; we may need to rely on the courts or law enforcement. We must decide if it is appropriate to restrain those intending or committing harm. There are no rote formulas: the decision is personal and situational.

You may act forcefully in self-defense while simultaneously offering an olive branch. You may employ force, in the least measure required, to halt destructive actions. At the same time, you may offer a hostile party an opportunity to collaborate on resolving major contentious issues. You may use force in a tit-for-tat manner: when the other party takes destructive action, you defend yourself vigorously, but when the other party is conciliatory, you extend positive concessions. While you are defending yourself, you communicate key principles of collaboration. In this way, you restrain the hostile party long enough to allow them to undergo a positive transformation.

On the other hand, if the reason you cannot walk away lies in your attachment to a particular outcome — whether that involves obtaining possessions you desire, teaching the other a lesson, defending your ego, or blind hatred and desire for revenge — you must sort out the factors that control your decisions and attachment.

❦

In what ways has this conflict served as a wake-up call?

Must you walk away from this conflict?

What valuable lessons will you take from this conflict if you must walk away?

Is it clear how you will avoid this type of situation in the future?

HEALING PERSONAL WOUNDS

While you may be able to resolve a conflict in the presence of unhealed emotional wounds, you will not be able to reconcile a relationship under such conditions. Relationship repair requires a deeper level of healing. Some mediators possess such skills; many do not.

Unhealed emotional wounds need not be the result of the present conflict; they may have been suffered previously, as it is not uncommon to find a party fighting old battles. They may have lost a prior contest of wills and they may be trying to make up for the defeat by picking a new fight they can win. When they realize the actual battle they are trying to resolve lies in earlier events (with people no longer present), the current conflict may resolve quickly.

Healing and catharsis are important when it comes to reconciling relationship. When you resolve conflict, catharsis and healing may take place naturally. However, when emotional wounds become barriers to resolution or reconciliation, you must carefully judge your ability to continue. A separate process designed specifically to heal emotional wounds may be needed. If the previous emotional trauma incapacitates you or the other party and renders either of you unable to participate, delay mediation until healing has taken place. Trauma care is not something a mediator provides; a mediator does not act as a therapist.

You might argue that most conflicts are rooted in psychological problems: if the other party had not been troubled, conflict would not have arisen. In this view, all conflict demands psychological remedies. For the purpose of mediation, however, the important factor is whether or not a party is in control of their current actions and decisions. Are they able to demonstrate self-determinism? If they can function in a self-determined manner, they can proceed with the process.

In some instances, emotional wounds may have so damaged a person that their relationships are constantly besieged by conflict. The unfortunate party who becomes entangled with them may be correct in asserting that healing the past must take precedence over mediation. However, if we honor self-determinism, we allow the troubled party, as much as possible, to dictate how they handle their past.

While these concerns are real, a more common danger is the tendency to treat normal responses to conflict as pathology. All parties involved in conflict suffer difficult moments: they experience turmoil; their self-image is challenged; they suffer anxiety and trepidation; and they grapple with disappointment. They are likely to face a wide range of human emotions. In mediation, we allow them to find their own strengths and truths, rather than labeling or diagnosing their feelings as mental illness, which aborts the opportunity for growth.

When a party experiences unusual trouble with difficult emotions, a mediator may narrow the discussion, setting aside issues requiring extensive healing of emotional wounds. Compartmentalizing the dispute in this manner allows the process to proceed.

In other cases, a mediator may anticipate that resolving the current conflict will aid in healing the past. He may observe that one party possesses qualities that will help the other party work through the conflict. For example, one party may possess a compassionate attitude that becomes the catalyst for healing. The subsequent resolution of a life problem (the conflict) may provide considerable benefit, including bolstering the confidence and optimism the challenged party needs in order to handle other interpersonal problems. Success in resolving the current conflict may thus indirectly heal wounds associated with past failures to handle conflict.

How will you determine if healing should be a part of this mediation?

Is it possible that this conflict is a proxy for an earlier conflict in your life?

In what way might you be fighting yesterday's battles?

Is it possible the other party is fighting an old battle?

Will it be necessary to separate issues in the present from issues concerning an earlier conflict?

Do you suspect the other party suffers from psychological problems that must be resolved before mediation will be successful?

Are there problems that should be addressed outside the mediation process?

Are you willing to postpone the process to give time for the other party to heal old wounds?

TWENTY-THREE

Closing

AT THIS STAGE, lessons learned find their final expression. Parties welcome the emerging future shaped by their settlement. If they rush to put the conflict behind them, they risk relegating the growth experienced to a mere footnote rather than a source of insights they can use to better their lives.

CELEBRATION OF RECONCILIATION

A ceremony or ritual may involve simple gestures performed with heightened importance and meaning. A signing of documents may be mundane in ordinary times but is elevated to a unifying ritual as mediation concludes. Parties may even stage a ceremony before stakeholders and the public to acknowledge success.

Metaphorically, this is the last section of the bridge you will travel to reconciliation. The bridge's final section is constructed using ritual acts that acknowledge the past and turn attention to the future. Creating the appropriate ceremony to acknowledge the end of a conflict is a matter of creativity. You may want to call on artists for symbolic means that can be used to tap deep emotions and sustain advances achieved in peacemaking.

Earlier, we compared the conflict resolution journey to the mythical hero's journey. We considered how we might see ourselves as characters in a personal heroic drama. This analogy is helpful once again. In ritual you step out of ordinary time and, in the language of the myth, you return from the other world (a realm of forgiveness and reconciliation) to the mundane world. The knowledge gained has a healing quality. In symbolic acts of ritual you demonstrate outwardly the inner lessons learned, culminating the hero's journey: "The old Self must be proven to be completely dead, and the new Self immune to temptations and addictions that trapped the old form."[1]

⚮

How might you demonstrate your satisfaction with reconciliation?

Describe a ritual that would best acknowledge the end of the conflict.

What symbolic acts might best represent letting go of the past?

What symbolic acts might best represent going from darkness to light, from conflict to harmony, from confusion to clarity?

What ritual might best acknowledge the transformation that took place?

FORMAL DOCUMENTS / PLATFORMS FOR CHANGE

A common ritual involves signing documents that capture the terms of a new agreement, which may consist of a simple paragraph or hundreds of pages with varying degrees of formality. While drafting a document may not rise to the level of ceremony mentioned earlier, capturing the intention of the parties accurately is an art form. Committing a shared vision of the future to written words can be done aesthetically. Capturing the heartbeat of a relationship in an agreement can be rewarding.

Settlement agreements usually include descriptions of remedies for a future breach, should one occur. Enforcement provisions describe what will take place if a party fails to meet their obligations. Addressing potential failures can be surprisingly positive; it allows you to jointly consider how to approach future conflict. At the conclusion of mediation, you are acutely aware of the wisdom of drafting provisions regarding future conflict, which may include clauses calling for mediation. Such provisions answer the question, "How will we manage differences in our relationship?"

As you become more and more aware of your interdependent nature and unique differences, you understand that the potential for conflict is a feature of life. For this reason, seek to put in place collaborative approaches to managing conflict.

Another purpose of a written agreement is to provide clarity that has been missing in the past. Clarity prevents future miscommunication, misunderstanding, or misguided expectations. Take the time to be certain your needs and expectations are clearly stated. Having just overcome conflict, you are acutely aware of the need for clear communication, intentions, and expectations. This should be reflected in the agreement.

Some might consider that formal written contracts are tedious, unnecessary, or even offensive; however, working on guidelines for the relationship demonstrates respect for self and others. When we view careful drafting of agreements as a form of caring for the other party's concerns as well as our own, those agreements become more than legalistic afterthought: they become a purpose-driven act of respect. The agreement becomes a blueprint for managing relationship in the days, months, and years to come.

A signing ceremony may serve as a symbolic event that endows the agreement with special meaning. If the task is not accomplished with creativity, the result can be an agreement that is too rigid to withstand future challenges. When you manage a relationship, it pays to focus on creating a flexible structure that serves you well into the future.

$\approx$

Will you need to formalize your agreement?

What terms will be needed to allow you to go forward with certainty?

What values should be reflected in the final agreement?

Is there a need to memorialize those who have suffered or sacrificed as a result of this conflict?

How you will fulfill the terms of the agreement?

What help will you require in drafting the agreement?

How will you monitor fulfillment of the terms?

Will performance benchmarks need to be clarified?

LESSONS LEARNED

Conflict might have been a warning, a knock on your door, announcing the need for personal growth. Your understanding of life may have been put on trial. A moment spent validating your new status will ensure you do not stumble and fall into old ways.

*

How might an artist represent changes that have taken place?

What have been the most important lessons learned?

If you were the hero in a mythic journey, what special knowledge did you acquire?

How will you keep fresh the lessons learned?

COMPASSION & UNCONDITIONAL LOVE

Previously, you came to accept conflict, discord, and struggle as reality. But after reconciliation, you know that life lived with compassion is the deepest reality possible. You know you must guard against all forces that seek to squeeze the love from your heart. You are not the person who entered the process; as a result, you need time to wear the skin of this "new person." You may feel ill at ease or worry that change will not endure. Ceremony and ritual acknowledge and celebrate the change from strife to harmony.

&

In the conflict resolution journey have you set aside a burden of hate? Describe.

Has compassion played a role in the outcome of this conflict?

GIVING THANKS

You may need to offer thanksgiving. When you celebrate reconciliation, you create an opportunity to show gratitude. Humility nurtured during conflict resolution becomes thanks offered to those who contributed to your transformation.

&

Describe assistance you received that made resolution possible.

Is thanks warranted?

Will gifts be exchanged?

CONFIDENTIALITY VERSUS PUBLIC NOTICE

In some instances, there are good reasons to maintain strict and extensive confidentiality. Confidentiality may have made a settlement possible; without such protection, you or the other party may have refused to reconcile. In some cases, confession and apology, if broadcast beyond the immediate parties, bring unnecessary censure and embarrassment. Thus, you must consider how you will balance the value of a public announcement with the value of confidentiality.

One component of forgiveness is willingness to no longer speak of the other party's transgressions. This tells us that transgressions should not be made a part of a public announcement. When one party appears to desire the public embarrassment of the other, reconciliation may not have taken place. On the other hand, a party's disclosure of their own transgressions offered as an act of contrition intended to bring about deeper reconciliation may be valuable. If one party has been publicly discredited as a result of the conflict, the other party's public accounting can restore the discredited person's public standing.

In some situations, public notice serves both the parties and the community and allows stakeholders to achieve closure. Upon achieving reconciliation, you can use shared celebration to alert stakeholders to cease hostility, as onlookers who previously took sides may be inclined to continue the conflict unless they have compelling reasons to accept and endorse the end of the conflict.

In addition, engaging in a reconciliation ceremony may provide stake-holders with catharsis that dissipates hostility, averting a resurgence of conflict. You will want to assess the degree to which stakeholders or spectators are in need of a symbolic release of tension and hostility and orchestrate a ceremony that satisfies their needs.

The community's desire for peace may have motivated you to seek mediation in the first place. Although confidentiality may have been part of the process, a public announcement thanking the community is in order.

Note that process confidentiality and post-settlement confidentiality differ — they are not the same. Public announcements can be crafted as shared statements of resolution and reconciliation that acknowledge the end of the conflict while omitting private information.

In the absence of such a joint statement, each party may agree not to disclose information, or they may negotiate a settlement clause that provides each party with the right to approve public statements made by the other party regarding the conflict. This may ensure the story presented to the public does not create confusion and misunderstanding. The same concerns arise when the audience is extended family.

Thus, a reconciliation ceremony or celebration that involves the larger public should be tailored to preserve needed confidentiality while providing public notice and drawing all affected by the conflict into restored harmony and new understanding.

How will you announce your reconciliation to stakeholders and the public?

Will you and the other party make a joint statement or separate statements?

What concerns do you have regarding public disclosure of the process and the outcome?

Will anything need to remain confidential?

Will you need to negotiate confidentiality provisions?

PUBLIC OPINION

The public is becoming increasingly sophisticated in the use of media; they will add their voices and become stakeholders in various conflicts. At times they may inadvertently promote additional conflict. Thus, you will want to be aware of how a conflict is perceived by public stakeholders, and you will want to be aware of how their participation affects the outcome.

When you plan reconciliation celebrations, you may want to consider how to interface with distant stakeholders who access the conflict through electronic media. If they are not included, they may intentionally or inadvertently fuel further conflict.

List stakeholders who will need to be informed.

What announcements will need to be issued?

How will the announcements affect your public image?

What role will public opinion play as you go forward?

Will you need to make sure the views of key stakeholders align with reconciliation?

TWENTY-FOUR

Closing Remarks

YOUR HARD WORK preparing for a facilitated negotiation has set the stage for your success. You are ready to reap the considerable dividends mediation preparation can deliver. Most likely you will arrive at a settlement agreement that provides greater satisfaction and is more enduring than outcomes you might have achieved otherwise.

Your goal may have been maximizing settlement terms, repairing valued relationships, or regaining the peace and contentment you had lost — now you are better prepared to reach that goal. In mediation, your success does not come at the expense of the other party; rather, both parties benefit from preparation. Benefits expand to the degree the other party also comes to the table understanding the process. You may even share the idea of preparing for mediation, inviting the other party to join you in preparing to seek the best possible resolution.

In addition, you are now prepared to collaborate with your attorney as a team. Ironically, it is your preparation that creates the best opportunity for your attorney to do his best work advocating on your behalf. Preparing for mediation increases your satisfaction with the client-attorney working relationship and reduces the stress connected with resolving a dispute. The enhanced attorney-client understanding improves a professional relationship that may continue long after this dispute is resolved. The possibility of misunderstanding that leads to ancillary disputes between counsel and client are greatly reduced.

As a bonus, your preparation provides insights that will help you anticipate and manage future conflict. You will be better prepared to prevent future escalation of conflict, thus avoiding expense and emotional stress. Learning how to prepare for mediation improves relationships; you will tend to experience less conflict and increased contentment and happiness.

May your life be blessed with the bounty of happiness that flows from an ability to maintain, protect, and restore the most valuable assets in your life: your relationships.

Notes

CHAPTER ONE

1. In many states, the law declares that all work product (notes, photos, data, sketches) prepared for the purpose of mediation shall be confidential and exempt from discovery during trial. Consult with your attorney regarding confidentiality provisions, as well as provisions regarding attorney-client privilege. If appropriate, you may wish to add the following to your journal: *"This material was prepared expressly and solely for the purpose of mediation and/or settlement conference. To the full extent provided by the law, the contents of this journal shall remain confidential and privileged."*

CHAPTER FOUR

1. In an *Early Neutral Evaluation*, a party presents their case to an attorney or retired judge who then provides an evaluation of the likely outcome at trial.

2. In a *Litigation Risk Analysis*, one creates a decision tree of all critical decisions in the life of the litigation and assigns a probability of success to each node. The cumulative probability is multiplied by the projected value of the case to arrive at a number that reflects the probable outcome. See: http://www.litigationrisk.com/

3. Discovery involves procuring information from the other party related to the litigation. It includes interrogatories, depositions, requests for admissions, and requests for production of documents or other evidence. Discovery can be time consuming and expensive.

4. Jonathan D. Glater, "Study Finds Settling is Better Than Going to Trial," *New York Times*, August 8th, 2008.

5. Robert F. Cochran Jr., John M. DiPippa, and Martha M. Peters, *The Counselor at Law: A Collaborative Approach to Client Interviewing and Counseling* (New York: Lexis Publishing, 1999), 1.

6. A mediation brief is a legal document drafted to inform the mediator regarding the facts of the case and applicable law. It provides a snapshot of the conflict, usually in legal terms. The mediation brief may address possible settlement scenarios.

CHAPTER FIVE

1. See: Kenneth Thomas, "Conflict and Conflict Management," *Handbook of Industrial and Organization Psychology* (Chicago: Rand McNally, 1976). Kenneth Thomas and Ralph Kilmann developed the "Thomas-Kilmann Conflict Mode Instrument." To access a self-scored test, see: https://kilmanndiagnostics.com.

2. Ibid.

CHAPTER SIX

1. A trial brief is defined as: "Counsel's written submission, usually just before trial, outlining the legal issues before the court and arguing one side's position." *Black's Law Dictionary* (St. Paul: West Group, 2001).

2. For a discussion of reshaping the stories we tell ourselves see: Sam Keen and Anne Valley-Fox, *Your Mythic Journey: Finding Meaning in Your Life Through Writing and Storytelling* (Los Angeles: Jeremy P. Archer, 1975 & 1989).

3. An exposition on the mythic archetypes that shape drama: Christopher Vogler, *The Writer's Journey*, 2nd ed. [Los Angeles: Michael Wiese Productions, 1998]

4. For a description of "funneling" and other interview techniques see: Cochran, DiPippa, and Peters, *The Counselor at Law*.

CHAPTER SEVEN

1. Thomas Jordan. *Glasl's Nine-Stage Model Of Conflict Escalation* (2000). See: https://www.researchgate.net/publication/265452970_Glasl's_Nine-Stage_Model_Of_Conflict_Escalation.

2. Ibid.

3. Deniable punishment is a covert harm done for which we can deny responsibility. For example, we can punish someone by tarnishing their relationship through covert gossip. See: Jordan, "Glasl's Nine Stage Model."

4. Ibid.

CHAPTER EIGHT

1. See: J.P. Folger, M.S. Poole, and R.K. Stutman, *Working Through Conflict: Strategies for Relationships, Groups, and Organizations*, 5th ed. (Boston: Pearson, 2005), 52.

2. Douglas Stone, Bruce Patton, and Sheila Heen, *Difficult Conversations: How to Discuss What Matters Most*, New York: Penguin Books, 1999, 106.

CHAPTER NINE

1. For a discussion of "I messages" see: Stone, Patton, and Heen, *Difficult Conversations*.

2. Ibid. 87

CHAPTER ELEVEN

1. Vivian C. Sheer and Michael F. Weigold, "Managing Threats to Identity:

The Accountability Triangle and Strategic Accounting," *Communication Research* 22.5 (October 1990), 595.

2. Ibid. 596

3. Ibid. 605

4. For more on the destructive third party see: ch. 11, "Managing Deception."

CHAPTER THIRTEEN

1. In the tit-for-tat strategy, if one party makes a competitive move, the other makes a competitive counter move; if one party makes a collaborative move, the other makes a collaborative move. This is a technique often used to educate the opposing party.

2. Laura Blumenfeld, *Revenge: A Story of Hope* (New York. Washington Square Press, 2003), 81.

CHAPTER FIFTEEN

1. The shift from positions to interests — the idea of going below the line — is covered in the groundbreaking work of Roger Fisher and William Ury, *Getting to Yes* (New York: Penguin Books, 1981).

2. Ibid. 18

CHAPTER SIXTEEN

1. Max H. Brazerman, "Negotiator Judgment: A Critical Look at the Rationality Assumption," 27 *Am. Beh. Sci.* 211 (1985): 211–24 in Charles B. Wiggins and L. Randolph Lowry, *Negotiation and Settlement Advocacy* (St. Paul, Minnesota: West Publishing, 1997) 141.

2. Dean G. Pruitt and Kim Sung Hee, *Social Conflict: Escalation, Stalemate, and Settlement*, 3rd ed. (Boston: McGraw Hill, 2004) 165.

3. Brazerman, "Negotiator Judgment," 137.

4. Ibid. 141

5. A BATNA is A Best Alternative to a Negotiated Agreement. See: Fisher and Ury, *Getting to Yes*.

CHAPTER SEVENTEEN

1. Harvard's Project on Negotiation offers some excellent titles, including: William Ury, *The Power of a Positive No: How to Say No and Still Get to Yes* (New York: Bantam Books, 2007), 5. See: also William Ury, *Getting Past No: Negotiating Your Way from Confrontation to Cooperation* (New York: Bantam Books, 1991) Fisher and Ury, *Getting to Yes*.

2. Robert O'Donnell of the Woodstock Institute for Negotiation has developed a protocol that guides a party through "the dance." Available at www.woodstockinstitute.com.

3. The previously cited protocol by O'Donnell can help determine a reasonable zone.

4. Gary Lowenthal, "Truthful Bargaining by Lawyers," in Charles B. Wiggins and L. Randolph Lowry, *Negotiation and Settlement Advocacy: A Book of Readings* (St. Paul, Minnesota: West Publishing, 1997), 269–271.

5. David A. Lax and James K. Sebenius, "Three Ethical Issues in Negotiation," in Charles B. Wiggins and L. Randolph Lowry, *Negotiation and Settlement Advocacy: A Book of Readings* (St. Paul, Minnesota: West Publishing, 1997), 276–279.

CHAPTER EIGHTEEN

1. O'Donnell, "A Different Look at Power" (unpublished paper, Woodstock Institute for Negotiation, Woodstock, Vermont, 1987), www.woodstockinstitute.com.

2. Ibid. 6

CHAPTER NINETEEN

1. Ibid.

2. Robert B. Cialdini, *Influence: Science and Practice*, 4th ed. (Boston: Allyn and Bacon, 2001).

CHAPTER TWENTY

1. For an excellent discussion of apology also see: Aaron Lazare, *On Apology*. (Oxford: Oxford University Press, 2004).

2. Jonathan R. Cohen, "Advising Clients to Apologize," *Southern California Law Review*, 72 (1999):1009.

CHAPTER TWENTY-ONE

1. Lewis B. Smedes, *Forgive and Forget: Healing the Hurts We Don't Deserve* (San Francisco: Harper Collins, 1984), 39.

CHAPTER TWENTY-THREE

1. Vogler, *The Writer's Journey*, 217.